EX LIBRIS

I hope this book proves
a blessing in your life,
and that you will see miracles
in 2006

Pat Robertson

MIRACLES
CAN BE YOURS TODAY

Pg-50-

Pg. 83-Angels

Pg 118-119. To 137 (MONeyS) Read 121 ALL

CHAPTER - Pg (121)

Pg 170 YeSHuA c8/10 DeSIRABLe Gifts

MIRACLES
CAN BE YOURS TODAY

Pat Robertson

INTEGRITY®
PUBLISHERS
Nashville

Library of Congress Cataloging-in-Publication Data
Robertson, Pat.
  Miracles / Pat Robertson.
    p. cm.
  Summary: "Helping 21st-century believers walk in the power of the Spirit and look past their "impossible" circumstances to all the possibilities of Almighty God"—Provided by publisher.
  Includes bibliographical references.
  ISBN 1-59145-423-9 (hardcover)
  1. Miracles.   I. Title.
BT97.3.R63   2006
231.7'3—dc22   2005031610

Printed in the United States of America
06 07 08 09 LBM 9 8 7 6 5 4 3 2 1

CONTENTS

ACKNOWLEDGMENTS

This is my seventeenth book, and I want to publicly thank my dear wife, Dede, who has shared with me a life of miracles for the past fifty-one years and who, as a voracious reader of books, has faithfully read and critiqued each chapter of this book, as well as the sixteen that preceded it.

I am old-fashioned and prefer to write using a pen and a legal pad. Words fail me to adequately thank my secretary G. G. Conklin, who not only is able to decipher my left-handed scrawl but remained boundlessly enthusiastic about the contents of each page and the opportunity to bring forth out of countless legal pads a finished, typed manuscript.

I owe a debt of gratitude to three extremely gifted CBN vice presidents—John Turver, Carol Ann Marshall, and Edie Wasserberg—who kept cheering me on in my predawn writing vigils.

I also want to acknowledge the CBN television producers who assembled for our television audience some of the thrilling stories of those whose lives had been touched by the hand of God—Kristi Watts and Ken Hulme, for the death to life story of Connie Davis; Gorman

ACKNOWLEDGMENTS

Woodfin, the miraculous tornado rescue of Kim and Evan Bernhardt; Ken Hulme and Amy Reid, the healing of Alan and Lisa Knupp's little baby; Rick Settoon, the creative miracle of Marlene Klepees; Debbie Harper, the story of Bob and Annie Arthur and the marriage from hell; Tim Branson, the story of Mark Gravell and the "checkmate" when the king had one more move; Kristen Cooney, the story of David Varon, whose blind eye became whole; Barbara Cornick, the story of Janet Taylor, the prostitute with addiction to crack cocaine; and Andrew Knox and Kristi Watts, the story of James Herring, who was freed from alcohol addiction.

Of course, I am grateful to the skilled team of sensitive literary professionals at Integrity Publishers—especially Byron Williamson, president and chief executive officer, and Joey Paul, senior vice president and publisher.

This book is dedicated to those men and women all over the world whose hearts are crying out to see in their lives the working of the miracle power of God.

INTRODUCTION

There is a longing in every human heart to feel that we are not alone in a vast imperial universe where distances are measured in billions of light years.

We worship. We bring gifts and offerings. We build temples, mosques, and churches. We bow down and cry out in hundreds of complex or simple rituals, all with one purpose: to demonstrate our belief in a being more powerful than we are, who is able to hear our supplication and then reach across the fathomless distances that surround us in order to guide us, comfort us, and take from us the dangers, diseases, and torments that are a part of our human existence.

Is all of this piety and religious zeal mere superstition? Is religion, as Karl Marx put it, merely the "opiate of the masses"? In short, is mankind's quest to be in touch with a higher power merely collective delusion, or is it based on concrete reality? Did a divine being create our vast universe and the inhabitants of our planet Earth, and does He now respond to the petitions of His creatures to bring them blessings and relief from their griefs and sufferings?

The critics either say there is no God (the atheists) or it is impossible to know anything about Him if indeed He exists (the agnostics). To them, our vast and complex universe arose from natural causes and over billions of years evolved into what exists today. Since to them a Creator does not exist, it is therefore folly and superstition to believe that worship of a divine being can bring any intervention in the lives of human beings today or at any time in history.

There are others whose beliefs make them neither atheists nor believers in the intervention of a divine being. To those whose beliefs place them under the heading "deists," God the Creator exists, but, like a supernatural watchmaker, He created the universe, assigned to it physical laws, wound it up like a watch, and then withdrew so that His creation could run on to infinity without any further intervention on His part. To the thoroughgoing deist, any interaction between God and man outside of the immutable natural laws is impossible.

Then there are Christian deists who believe that God has intervened in human affairs in a manner described in the pages of the Old and New Testaments, but these interventions were in accordance with specific "dispensations." To the dispensationalist, the age of God's specific demonstration of miraculous power toward humanity ended with the death of the last of the apostles of Jesus Christ. Thereafter was the Church Age, during which, they say, the Christian church was guided by the inspired Holy Scriptures without the supernatural interventions of God that had characterized the days of the apostles.

Despite the naysayers, there is a vastly larger number of people who believe in a power or powers beyond the realm of human intellect that cannot be known by the senses of seeing, hearing, touch, taste, or smell. To these people, there is a "secret kingdom" of vast potential that transcends human thought and ability. This is the realm of the spirit . . . the realm of the miraculous.

Introduction

The purpose of this book is to show to you, the reader, beyond any doubt, not only the realm of the miraculous but the real-life stories of people who have experienced miracles in our modern day. Then I want to show you in simple terms what Jesus Christ, the Son of God, told His disciples about how they could experience miracles in their lives and ministries. For you, these will become the keys to open for you an entrance into the miraculous.

The dictionary defines *miracle* as "a marvelous event manifesting a supernatural act of God." The Easton's *1897 Bible Dictionary* expands the concept as follows:

> An event in the external world brought about by the immediate agency or the simple volition of God, operating without the use of means capable of being discerned by the senses. It is an occurrence at and above nature and above man. It shows the intervention of a power that is not limited by the laws either of matter or of mind, a power interrupting the fixed laws which govern their movements, a supernatural power. . . . God ordinarily effects his purpose through the agency of second causes; but he has the power also of effecting his purposes immediately and without the intervention of second causes, i.e. of invading the fixed order, and thus of working miracles.

Allow me now to introduce you to soul-stirring accounts of miracles in the lives of everyday people and the biblical basis upon which these miracles rest.

HE WALKED ON WATER

The Bible tells us that late one afternoon, Jesus Christ went up into the hills of Galilee by Himself to pray. Before He did so, He instructed His disciples to get into a boat and row across the turbulent Sea of Galilee to the other shore. As daylight faded into darkness, the disciples were struggling with their oars, only halfway across the choppy sea. Then, suddenly, Jesus came to them . . . walking on the water.

When the ever-impetuous Simon Peter saw Jesus walking on the water, he called out, "Lord, if it is You, command me to come to You on the water." Jesus responded, "Come."

Hearing that command, Simon Peter sat on the side of the boat, lowered himself over the edge, and began to walk on the water. This spontaneous miracle took place in a matter of seconds, and it ended abruptly. As soon as Peter became fully aware of what he was doing, his rational self took over and shouted to his subconscious, "You can't walk on water! You are going to sink and drown!" As soon as this negative thought came, he began to sink beneath the stormy water.

At that moment, Jesus reached out, grasped Peter's hand, and pulled him up. Then, miraculously, Peter was safe in the boat.

Did Jesus congratulate Peter for having enough faith to step out of a safe boat into a deep and stormy sea in the middle of the night and begin to walk on water? Not at all. His only comment was curt and to the point: "O you of little faith, why did you doubt?" (see Matthew 14:22–31).

Peter had obeyed the Lord's command; he had committed his body to very deep waters and had actually done what no human, other than Jesus Himself, had ever done—he walked on water! Yet because Peter allowed his rational mind to create fear instead of faith, Jesus hurled a term of scorn at him: "you of little faith."

So we observe that big faith enables us to walk on water, while little faith causes us to sink. Faith can indeed suspend the laws of nature so that a human body, which is denser than water, can, in fact, become so light that its footsteps do not penetrate the water. Instead, for the person of faith, the water becomes a firm pathway.

If this is indeed true, then we must ask ourselves two questions: What is faith? And faith in what or whom? The Bible gives us the answers to both questions.

WHAT IS FAITH?

Faith, we are told in Hebrews 11:1, is the title deed to things we have hoped for and the evidence of things we have not yet seen. Let's examine each of these aspects of faith more closely.

The Title Deed of Things Hoped For

How does a title deed work? Assume for a moment that the owner of a farm offers to sell it to you. You like what you have heard and agree to purchase the farm, sight unseen, at the specified price. You write a check, and the farm owner signs over to you a properly notarized title

2

deed, which transfers ownership of the farm to you. Assuming no other conditions, the title deed gives you all of the privileges and rights of ownership to the farm. You can live on it, grow crops on it, raise livestock on it, plant trees on it, explore it for minerals, build barns on it, dig a fishing pond on it, rent it to tenants, subdivide it, or sell it. By the title deed, you have all these rights—yet you, if you so desired, would never have to set foot on or even see the farm. You have the title deed!

The title deed to the farm not only entitles you to a host of wonderful privileges, but it also brings responsibilities. The crops have to be tended, the livestock fed and watered, the forests managed, the houses and barns painted and repaired, and the land maintained according to the laws of man and nature.

In a similar way, faith is the title deed to the hopes and dreams that God has placed in our hearts. Inside each of us who knows Him is a destiny, along with all the rights, privileges, and responsibilities that accompany that destiny. Faith brings the privileges of material provision, healings, miracles, and blessings that accompany ownership of your God-ordained destiny. But faith also brings you the responsibility to keep the garden of your life free from weeds; to nourish your mind, soul, spirit, and body; and to care diligently for the people and material possessions that, over the years, become part of your destiny.

The Evidence of Things Not Seen

Faith, according to Hebrews 11:1, is "the evidence of things not seen." What does this mean?

Years ago, I learned in my high school physics class that what seemed to be solid, visible matter was, in fact, invisible energy. The brilliant theoretical physicist Albert Einstein proposed the remarkable formula that forever changed our perception of the physical universe: $E=MC^2$.

According to Einstein, matter and energy are essentially part of the same thing, and when a uranium atom is properly bombarded with electrons, the energy released is so enormous that it is calculated as the mass of the uranium multiplied by the speed of light squared—hence, the incredible explosive force of the atomic bomb and the hydrogen bomb.

The power of the invisible world of the spirit ("things not seen") is beyond calculation. We live in the visible world. We describe this visible world in terms of its limitations. Human beings are called "mortal" because we all live subject to death (in Latin, *mort*). There are limits to what we can do, so we say our horizons are "finite." Our food quickly decays, so we say it is "perishable." Our thought processes are subject to error, so we say we are "fallible." We easily fall into sin, so we say we are "corruptible."

On the other hand, theologians who have tried to describe God use terms that indicate the absence of human limitations. God is "immortal," "infinite," "infallible," and "incorruptible." Or they say that God is the sum of all human capabilities: We are powerful; God is all-powerful. We have some knowledge; God has all knowledge. We are limited in time and space; God is present everywhere.

Therefore, faith is a window into an invisible, "not seen" world where there are no physical limitations. There is no sickness, no disease, no death, no poverty, no failure, and no hatred or discord. It is a world of the spirit where there is perfect knowledge and no limitations of time and space. Granted, only One, who was sinless, could see it perfectly; we sinners, like the apostle Paul, "see through a glass, darkly" (1 Corinthians 13:12 KJV). Nevertheless, nothing should stop us from asking God to give us faith in the "things not seen" and then appropriating the incredible realm of the invisible, where all things are possible.

He Walked on Water

Where should our faith be centered? Should it be on ourselves and our abilities? Should it be on the circumstances that surround our lives? Should it be on our physical or financial strength?

In what I consider the best summary of how to receive miracles, found in Mark 11:12–25, Jesus tells us simply, "Have faith in God" (v. 22).

But in *what* God should we have faith? British scholar J. B. Phillips wrote a book entitled *Your God Is Too Small* (Touchstone, 2004), in which he recalled asking a group of students during World War II if they believed that God understood radar. The almost unanimous answer was that no, God (who, by the way, put radar in the flying bat) did not understand radar.

I remember several years ago reading the results of a national survey taken in the United States dealing with God and heaven. Of those surveyed, fully 90 percent thought that they were going to heaven when they died, yet only about half that number thought their neighbors were going to heaven. About 65 percent thought that celebrities such as Oprah Winfrey, Colin Powell, Michael Jackson, and Princess Diana were going to heaven, while less than 50 percent felt that certain Christian ministers, including this author, who had spent their lives preaching the gospel of Jesus Christ would go to heaven.

In short, the popular perception of God is fatally flawed. God is not an old man in a rocking chair way up in the heavens, hopelessly out of touch with modern life. Nor is He keeping score for rewards and punishment according to the fleeting whims and fashions of contemporary pop culture.

The God of the Bible is a God of love. He knows everything and experiences everything. He knows our needs before we ask Him

(Matthew 6:8). Not only does He keep track of every bird in the sky (v. 26), but His records about you and me are so incredibly complete that He has an inventory of each hair on our heads and every second of our lives from the moment we are born to the moment we die (Psalm 139:16; Matthew 10:30).

Far from being a doddering old man, the Ancient of Days is an eternal spirit who is forever young. My friend, the late Father Dennis Bennett, had a unique description of God's age that I have never forgotten: "We have sinned and grown old. Our Father is younger than we."

It is a sobering fact to realize that God Almighty, the eternal spirit who has been in existence "from everlasting to everlasting" (Psalm 90:2), is, in fact, younger than I am. His name, *Jehovah*, is taken from the Hebrew verb "to be." God is being itself. He is life itself. He never grows weary (Isaiah 40:28). He neither slumbers nor sleeps (Psalm 121:3). He is fully aware of everything that happens in the universe. He is never caught off guard or surprised, because He knows the end from the beginning of all things (Isaiah 46:10). He is able to control all things.

GOD'S POWER REVEALED IN CREATION

Just for a moment, consider God's infinite power and wisdom. I was told by a brilliant Jewish astrophysicist that the best scientific thinkers, using the most advanced telescopes and computers, have determined that our universe began fifteen billion years ago when an extraordinarily dense collection of energy and mass exploded in what has come to be known as the "big bang." From that occurrence, hot gases and other material thrust outward in all directions at speeds approaching the speed of light to form an ever-expanding universe containing at least one hundred million galaxies, each similar to the Milky Way, of which our solar system makes up merely a small part.

But the story doesn't end there. According to this astrophysicist, who is a graduate of MIT and a distinguished scientist, a sizeable core of scientists agree that our vast universe is, in his own words, "tuned for life." He astounded our CBN television audience by claiming that if the amount of material in the "big bang" had varied by a factor of ten followed by twenty-six zeros—essentially a fly speck in the universe— the conditions would not have been suitable for life on planet Earth!

Can you or I even contemplate a Being with intelligence and power so infinite that He could calculate the precise amount of material needed over fifteen billion years to exert a balanced gravitational pull that would prevent the universe from either flying apart or, in turn, collapsing upon itself? And, in the process, positioning a tiny planet with just enough mass and moisture in an exact orbit around a blazing star to give it the right amount of light and heat, day and night? To create, in fact, an ideal environment for plant and animal life, as well as a suitable home for a race of beings created in the image of God?

I stand in awe at the varieties of plants, fruits and vegetables, fish, birds, and other animals that God has placed on this earth. We can only marvel at the complex and beautiful laws of nature and the exquisite balance of the seasons, the oceans and rivers, the winds, the rains, and the magnetic forces at work in our planet.

This book obviously isn't intended to be even a cursory study of science, but let's look at a simple example of God's amazing order in creation, so that it can bring us to a closer understanding of the One upon whom our faith must rest.

Consider just one of God's marvels—ice. When most substances freeze, they take up *less* space, making them denser than their liquid form. That's why most solids sink. But when water freezes, it actually expands, taking up *more* space. Because ice is lighter than the same amount of liquid water, it does not sink. Instead, it floats, allowing the water beneath it to remain liquid.

Imagine what would happen to marine life if ice in freezing weather sank to the bottom of the water, followed by more ice, and more ice until the rivers and freshwater lakes were frozen solid. All of the fish would die, and no water would be available for man or animal. Why is it this way? Because that's exactly how a wise God created it.

GOD'S POWER REVEALED IN THE CHURCH

When Jesus Christ came to earth, He was aware of God's enormous power. That is why He boldly declared, "With God all things are possible" (Matthew 19:26). This is why He told His disciples to have faith in God (Mark 11). This is why He cried out in disgust when His disciples failed to cast a demon out of a little child (Matthew 17:17). Jesus was fully aware of the awesome knowledge and power of His heavenly Father. He saw it clearly and simply, and He seemed genuinely disturbed that the disciples whom He loved could not see what He saw or do what He did.

In fact, He told them before His crucifixion, "He who believes in Me, the works that I do he will do also; and greater works than these he will do, because I go to My Father" (John 14:12). In our day, we who are His disciples should also expect to do what Jesus did when He was here on earth. In fact, He promised for us even greater things than He did. For twenty-first century followers of Christ, a life filled with miracles should be the norm, not the exception.

Two things are abundantly evident. First, Scripture reveals that Almighty God, the Creator of the universe and all that is in it, has the power to bring forth miracles for those who have faith in Him. Second, it is equally clear from the life and teachings of Jesus Christ, the Son of

God, that authority and power to perform miracles have been given to Christian believers until the "end of the age" (Matthew 28:20).

Jesus sent His disciples throughout Israel to heal the sick and cast out demons. After His resurrection, He told His disciples to wait in Jerusalem until they had received "power from on high" (Luke 24:49). Then they were to go to the entire world and teach all nations to obey everything He had told them (Matthew 28:19–20; Acts 1:8). To them, fully preaching the gospel, in the words of the apostle Paul, was with "signs and wonders and mighty deeds" (2 Corinthians 12:12).

The early church and the apostles did exactly what Jesus had told them. They preached in power and led multitudes to faith. They were empowered by the Holy Spirit of God; and they raised the dead, healed the sick, cast out demons, and, in a short time, "turned the world upside down" (Acts 17:6). In truth, no greater miracle exists than the amazing growth of the Christian church from a terrified band of 120 uneducated men and women to a 2.2 billion-member religion, the largest in the world today.

GOD'S POWER REVEALED IN MIRACLES

In the year 1900, a humble pastor and Bible teacher in Topeka, Kansas, named Charles Parham began praying with a handful of students to receive from God the same experience of the baptism of the Holy Spirit that had fallen on the early Christians on the day of Pentecost. In answer to the study, prayers, and earnest entreaties of this tiny band of students and their professor, God Almighty began the twentieth century with an outpouring of the Holy Spirit remarkably similar to what happened in an upper room in Jerusalem on the day of Pentecost in the early years of the first century.

Charles Parham's granddaughter, Bobi Hromas, is a valued member of the board of trustees of Regent University, of which I am the founder and chancellor. During an informal dinner of our trustees, Bobi told us about the miracle of Topeka, Kansas. Her grandfather had assigned to his students a project to discover from the Bible how the power of the Holy Spirit came upon the early Christians and what happened to them so that they would know they had been baptized in the Holy Spirit according to Jesus's command to "tarry in . . . Jerusalem" until they had received "power from on high" (Luke 24:49).

As Bobi told it, the students gathered back together after a couple of weeks of intensive study. They were in unanimous agreement: the biblical evidence of the baptism of the Holy Spirit was the *glossolalia*, or speaking in tongues, under the direction of the Holy Spirit.

Since none of the students at the Topeka, Kansas, school or their teacher had received the biblical experience, they debated among themselves who would be the "guinea pig" among them to be their object of prayer. The students suggested Bobi Hromas's grandfather, Charles Parham, but he replied, "I am not holy enough to receive this blessing. Select someone else."

So the students selected one of their classmates, gathered around her, and laid their hands on her. Then they prayed and cried out to God that He would baptize their friend and fellow student with the Holy Spirit as He baptized the earlier believers on the day of Pentecost.

God responded to their faith, and a miracle took place. The power of God descended upon the young student, and she was filled with the glorious power of the Holy Spirit. From the depths of her being, she poured forth a language unknown to any in the group. For hours, her spirit was communing with the Holy Spirit, and her mouth was speaking prayer and praise in a language that the group finally recognized as Chinese.

Word of this remarkable miracle reached the local paper, and a reporter was sent to get an interview. Unfortunately, to each question that was put to the young student in English, she answered in fluent Chinese. Frustrated, the reporter tried to conduct the interview in writing. So he asked his questions in English and requested the student to write the answers on a piece of paper. And write she did . . . in perfect Chinese script! (I have seen a photograph of the original, which the Parham family retained as a prized possession.)

The miracle of Topeka, Kansas, did not stop there, because many others came to receive the Pentecostal blessing. One such supplicant was an African-American named James Seymour, who traveled to Los Angeles, California, and held meetings in a livery stable at a location that soon became famous, Azusa Street. What became known as the Azusa Street revival launched the fastest-growing expression of any religion in history, the Pentecostal-charismatic movement, which grew from one Bible teacher and a handful of students in 1900, to six hundred million people worldwide at the turn of the twentieth century, and is projected to grow to one billion by the year 2020.

With the power of the Holy Spirit has come a veritable cascade of miraculous events—the dead have been raised, millions of people have been miraculously healed, demons have been cast out, miraculous financial provision has come, corrupt governments have been toppled and righteous leaders put in their place, and time and again God's people have been rescued from life-threatening peril.

Such is the miraculous true story of Kim Bernhardt, a single mom, and her four-year-old son.

GOD'S POWER REVEALED THROUGH FAITH

I witnessed firsthand the terrible devastation brought about by Hurricane Hugo, which struck Charleston, South Carolina; Hurricane Andrew, which devastated Homestead, Florida; and Hurricane Katrina, which struck the Gulf Coast with such force that it was the worst natural disaster in United States history. I led relief efforts and television coverage of these and other disasters, and, frankly, words fail me to express the extent of the devastation and human suffering that these storms have caused.

But for sheer terror, not even a hurricane can compare to the concentrated fury of a monster tornado with winds swirling in excess of two hundred miles per hour in a black, concentrated vortex of destruction. Anything caught in the grasp of one of these monsters is lifted violently in the air and then smashed back to earth. Buildings in their paths are reduced to rubble and splinters.

September 20, 2002, dawned clear and peaceful in the Indianapolis area. Kim Bernhardt and her four-year-old son, Evan, went out in their white minivan to pick up a few items at a local home-improvement store. While they were there, the clear skies turned ominous, and local radio stations began broadcasting thunderstorm warnings with tornado sightings in the area. The weather situation rapidly turned critical, and the home-improvement store where Kim was shopping urged its patrons to leave and seek suitable shelter from what could be dangerous thunderstorms and life-threatening tornadoes.

Kim did not panic but calmly buckled her child into his car seat in the minivan and began a three-block drive to their church, where Kim felt they would have adequate shelter. But Kim did not reckon with the devilish speed of the twister that was roaring down on their neighborhood. She hurried to safety, but she was too late. Just as she rounded the corner into the church parking lot, the monster was upon her. In an instant, it picked up the minivan, with Kim and Evan still inside, and hurled them straight up in the air! Up and up they went until the minivan was held level but spinning around some ten feet above the telephone poles along the road.

Death seemed imminent. A sudden crash from that height would surely destroy the minivan and snuff out the lives of Kim and her child. Yet Kim didn't panic. Something like a supernatural presence came upon her. First, she thought of Evan, so she dove into the back and put Evan on the floor. As she peeked out of the window of the van, she could see houses beneath her being sucked apart by the twister.

Kim knew her only hope was faith in God and His miraculous power. In faith, she began to pray a prayer she had learned as a child, the Lord's Prayer: "Our Father, which art in heaven . . . Thy will be done on earth as it is in heaven." As she prayed, a thought came to her—a thought that she later realized had come from her Father in heaven: *Put the van in park.* To a person flying in a tornado fifty feet in the air, the gearing of a minivan was illogical, counterintuitive, the last thing in the world with which to be concerned. But Kim obeyed the voice. She reached forward and put the gear lever in park. Then she sheltered little Evan and silently prayed.

Suddenly, quietly and gently, as if it was being cradled by a giant hand, the minivan settled to earth upright on its four wheels about three blocks from where it had become airborne. They came to earth about fifty feet from a house. Kim quickly realized that had the van with its engine still running been in gear, it would have lurched forward into the house with probably great damage and physical harm. As it was, her windshield was cracked, the rear windows were blown out, and the interior of the car was covered with debris. But Kim and Evan walked out of the vehicle without a scratch. Remarkably, her only loss was one earring.

Once on the ground, Kim looked around to see devastation everywhere. Houses were torn apart and trees ripped from their roots. But Kim and Evan were safe.

Hours later, Kim was still in shock as she relayed her story to people in the neighborhood. No one could believe that she and Evan walked away without a scratch, although eyewitnesses testified to seeing the white minivan airborne, sailing above the telephone poles.

Kim still talks about how real God's presence was in the midst of the terrifying twister. "That prayer has a different meaning to me now: 'Thy will be done on earth as it is in heaven,'" she says. She realized that she was literally suspended between heaven and earth. The earth was being torn apart by the twister, but Kim knows that the God of heaven was right there with her, cradling her van "gently—and I mean *gently*" in His hands.

Looking back, Kim says her darkest moment came when she thought that Evan might be killed by the tornado while she survived. As the minivan twirled in the air, she knew that she was staring death in the face. "Yet there was peace," she says. "I knew I was in the hands of God. He loves us so much, and I never felt it more than in that tornado."

She remembers the words of the prophet Nahum: "The LORD has His way in the whirlwind and in the storm" (1:3). She says, "He was in the whirlwind. He was with us. I feel like He proved His love to me. I know He did it a long time ago on the cross, but He showed me that day how much He loved me."

Kim says she learned lasting spiritual lessons from her ordeal. "He used that storm to prepare me for other situations that have come up in my life. It was going through that storm that has given me the faith to hold on."

INCREASE OUR FAITH

One day, Jesus's disciples, who had been witnessing their leader performing great miracles of faith every day, came to Him with this very understandable and seemingly simple request: "Increase our faith" (Luke 17:5).

Jesus's reply was abrupt and perplexing: "If you had faith as small as a mustard seed you could say to this mountain, 'Move from here to there,' and it would move. Nothing would be impossible" (Matthew 17:20 NLT).

A mustard seed is tiny, hardly bigger than a grain of sand. Jesus had told Peter that he was "of little faith" because he could not walk on water. Jesus was angry because His disciples could not heal a demon-possessed boy who was manifesting symptoms of epilepsy (Matthew 17:14–18). Now He tells them that access to miraculous, earth-moving power was available to them if they had faith no bigger than a tiny seed.

But whose faith was Jesus referring to: the faith of the disciples or the faith that comes from God? I believe that it was the latter.

Without question, human beings working in harmony can accomplish spectacular feats. At the ancient tower of Babel, God Himself declared, "Indeed the people *are* one and they all have one language . . . now nothing that they propose to do will be withheld from them" (Genesis 11:6).

With enough time and the appropriate tools, human beings working together can dig down a mountain and transport it into the sea. In fact, they did just that at the new international airport in Hong Kong. The tunnels, the bridges, the railways, the highways, the skyscrapers, the factories, the giant drills, the bulldozers, the loaders, the two-hundred-ton trucks, the rockets, and the satellites—all bear witness to what men, corporations, and nations can accomplish. Those who build such marvels certainly dwell in a realm of faith and human ability. In that sense, what human beings have accomplished through perseverance, intelligence, skill, and teamwork is nothing short of miraculous.

Yet Jesus was speaking not of the miracles of human endeavors, but the miracles that come about by human beings who are filled with the faith of the Creator. Remember, the Creator had the power to bring the entire universe into existence merely by speaking it so. Human endeavor can accomplish much, but nothing we can do in our strength can in any way compare to the strength of the One who spans eternity and sustains not just our planet, but our solar system, our galaxy, and our entire universe.

If a man or woman were to be given the tiniest portion of God's faith, that individual would be able to shake the world. No living human could handle an "increased" portion of God's faith, for with it he or she could move the stars out of their orbits.

So Jesus urges His disciples to have faith, even if it was only as big as a mustard seed. Was such a thing possible, or was Jesus merely tantalizing His disciples with an unattainable ideal? I, for one, believe that an impartation of God's faith is possible—and with it, extraordinary miracles can take place.

I want to make it abundantly clear that I am not talking about working up faith. I am not talking about religious exercises that somehow bring on faith. I am certainly not talking about magic incantations, spells, or superstitious rituals. I am talking about a supernatural impartation of God's Holy Spirit to those who are willing to receive Him for the purpose of bringing forth supernatural faith. A story from my own experience illustrates what I am talking about.

MIRACLES INCREASE OUR FAITH

In 1956, while I was in business in New York City, I received Jesus Christ as my Savior and was gloriously born again. I felt that there was a call on my life to serve Him. After much prayer, I enrolled for theological education at Biblical Seminary (later renamed New York Theological Seminary) to begin a three-year course that later led to a master of divinity degree.

While at seminary, I joined in earnest and extended prayer with fellow students and a couple of area ministers. I wanted the Lord to baptize me with His Holy Spirit. One evening in the fall of 1958, my oldest son fell ill and became unconscious, burning with a fever. I knelt beside him, begging God to heal him. Then the Holy Spirit stopped me and showed me that my heavenly Father loved this little boy thousands of times more than I did. I stopped begging and beseeching, and I consciously surrendered my little boy into the care of his loving heavenly Father. As I did so, the power of God enveloped him and the fever broke. He regained consciousness, got up, and, after a restful night's sleep, was totally healed from any effects of the virus that had attacked him.

I was so grateful that I began to pour out praise and thanksgiving to the God who had performed this miracle before my very eyes. As I was praising and thanking the Lord, I found that something deep within me was given a voice, and I began praying and thanking the Lord in what sounded like an African dialect. While I had been worshiping the Lord for His goodness, He responded by giving me what I had been asking for during the previous two years: the baptism of the Holy Spirit!

I could fill many books with things that happened after that wonderful night. Suffice it to say, I moved into the Book of Acts. I entered the realm of miraculous power, and, almost fifty years later, I haven't looked back.

When I graduated from seminary in 1959, I began seeking God in earnest to find out His plan for the rest of my life. I drove my family from New York to my parents' home in Lexington, Virginia. While there, my mother received a letter from George Lauderdale, a high school friend with whom I had not been in contact for at least seventeen years. The letter from my friend, who had followed in his father's footsteps and entered the ministry, contained this cryptic line: "There is an abandoned television station in Portsmouth, Virginia. Would Pat be interested in claiming it for the Lord?"

This proposal seemed outlandish, since I didn't even own a television set, much less a television station. Yet I had been asking God for direction, and I was open to His leading.

Several days later, I drove to the downtown of this lovely Southern college town and stopped at the post office. Imagine my surprise when the gaunt figure of George Lauderdale appeared at my car window. I greeted him warmly and learned that the night before he had a dream instructing him to drive from Norfolk, Virginia, across the state to Rockbridge County because, according to the dream, "his work in Rockbridge was not finished." He had just completed a five-hour drive, and his arrival in downtown Lexington precisely intersected my stop at the Lexington post office.

He then drove with me to WREL, the local AM radio station where

I was doing a fifteen-minute devotional broadcast sponsored by a local Christian businessman. George began telling me about this small UHF television station on Channel 27 that had just stopped broadcasting and was now for sale. Over my protests about my total inexperience in this line of work (I hadn't even taken a course in audiovisual presentations), George explained how easy it was and assured me that if God was in it, everything would work out fine. I learned more about the station, found out the name and address of the owner, and promised to pray about it.

Here I was, a recent seminary graduate with a wife, three little children, no job, and almost no money, talking about buying a defunct television station. To the rational mind, the proposition was ludicrous, but the Bible tells us that "the foolishness of God is wiser than man's wisdom" (1 Corinthians 1:25 NIV).

My parents' home adjoined a high school nestled in a little valley beside a stream called Woods Creek. Next to the high school was a tiny football field where I had played football during the one year I spent at Lexington High School. That night, I walked over to the football field, and, under the stars of a clear Shenandoah Valley night, I talked to my heavenly Father. "If this thing is of You, Father," I prayed, "how much will the station cost?" Immediately a figure came into my mind: $37,000. Along with the number came a peace that this enterprise was of God.

For a step of this magnitude, a great deal more confirmation was needed! I left Lexington, Virginia, and drove my wife and children to her parents' home in Columbus, Ohio. Then I drove back to our apartment in Queens, New York.

There I isolated myself with my Bible and with the Lord. Day after day, I poured out my heart to Him. But my only clear direction was a command given by Jesus to a rich young ruler who had come to Him asking for advice: "Sell everything you have and give to the poor. . . . Then come, follow me" (Luke 12:33, 18:22 NIV).

I contacted my wife at her parents' home in Ohio with the news that I had received clear direction from the Lord. She replied, "You do what the Lord tells you." With that green light, I put an ad in the Woodside, Queens, paper, advertising "Early American-style furniture for sale." Soon our small apartment was overrun with buyers who eagerly bought everything we had except some wedding presents, the children's beds, and our kitchen pots and pans.

I then contacted Dick Simmons, a classmate and Presbyterian minister who had taken the pastorate of the Classen Avenue Presbyterian Church and was living in its brownstone parsonage, located in the heart of Bedford Stuyvesant, considered by many the second-worst slum in New York. The parsonage adjoined another brownstone, which was owned by a black madam who was running a bordello there.

Dick assured me that we could move in with him temporarily, so I gave up the lease on our very desirable apartment, packed up the pots and pans and the children's beds, and moved to the parsonage on Classen Avenue in "Bed-Sty." Then I gave Dick Simmons the proceeds from the sale of our furniture to give to the poor who lived nearby.

A few days later, my wife called and, with a frantic voice, said, "Our phone has been disconnected, and my call was transferred to Brooklyn. What in the world is going on?"

I replied calmly, "I told you that the Lord was speaking to me out of Luke 12:33, and you said to go ahead. So I sold our furniture and moved in with Dick and Barbara Simmons."

"You what?" she sobbed. "You sold our furniture! I didn't know what Luke 12:33 said, and I didn't look it up. What have you done?!"

I assured her that I would drive out to Ohio to get her and the children and that I felt God was getting us ready to travel light to follow His plan for us. To say that my lame explanation even came close to easing her shock would be a gross overstatement. Despite all that turmoil, we moved into the parsonage in Brooklyn a few weeks later.

Looking back on our ordeal in the parsonage, I laughingly tell audiences that I once lived in an interracial commune "before communes were cool." In that house we had the ex-madam from next-door, a slightly feeble-minded black giant from one of the Caribbean islands, and a severely cerebral-palsied man who was a recipient of the largess of opera singer Jerome Hines and who, I might add, had an uncontrollable sex drive that resulted in the pregnancy of his equally handicapped girlfriend.

In the mix were Dick and Barbara Simmons and their severely brain-damaged baby boy, assorted characters from the streets of New York (some holy and some unholy), and, of course, my wife Dede and me, along with our three red-haired, blue-eyed, fair-skinned clearly Anglo-Saxon children living in a community that was 99 percent African-American.

I was still looking for the clear leading of the Lord, but something was blocking the next step. In desperation, I came upon a seemingly virtuous solution. My wife and I would somehow find the way to purchase the brownstone (former bordello) next-door. It was now empty because the madam, having missed the payments on her real-estate contract, had been evicted. We would begin a spiritual mission to the people in that community who were spiritually and materially needy.

The spiritual breakthrough came when my dear wife, who, up to this point, had felt that my spiritual detour from seeming rationality into the depths of this spiritually charged Brooklyn commune was clearly delusional, now looked me in the eyes and said with great sincerity, "If you feel that the Lord wants us to buy that house and stay in Brooklyn to minister to these people, I am with you!"

Did God want me to purchase the former bordello and begin an urban ministry to the needy folks in Bed-Sty? As I prayed about the matter, the Holy Spirit spoke to me with great clarity: "Read Jeremiah 16:2." I quickly opened my Bible and read some of the most welcome words I had ever seen in my life: "You shall not take a wife, nor shall you have sons or daughters in this place."

I practically shouted for joy! Now, almost fifty years later, I can understand what had happened. First, I had surrendered my meager material possessions in obedience to the Lord's command. Then my wife had willingly joined me in offering our lives and our concept of a future good life to live among the poor and downtrodden in order to serve them.

Like the test of obedience given to Abraham some four thousand years ago, without fully realizing the significance of what was taking place, we had been given two tests of obedience and had passed them both.

Now God was prepared to give me a revelation of His plan for my life and, along with the plan, an impartation of His faith that I would need through the succeeding years to bring about the work that He had set out for me and that He had determined would impact the entire world.

With the Brooklyn door closed, I needed a serious time of prayer. I took a sleeping bag, several cans of fruit juice, and my Bible over to the creaky, nineteenth-century Classen Avenue Presbyterian Church, where I spent seven days seeking God's direction for my life.

As I spent the week in prayer, the Lord made it clear that I was to possess the rundown television station in Portsmouth, Virginia. But God's plan far transcended one little station in one medium-sized area.

There was to be a network of stations covering most of the United States. I was thinking airborne television, which was the only television technology used in field tests in 1959 able to cover large distances. But God was thinking of a technology not yet born: satellite television.

God's word came to pass twenty years later, when the ministry that the Lord led me to form, the Christian Broadcasting Network, became the first religious organization in history to have its own twenty-four-hour satellite transponder capable of spanning the United States of America and surrounding territories. In 1977, the Christian Broadcasting Network became one of only three broadcasters in the United States to lease full-time television transponders on the RCA Satcom I satellite. One year later, we launched America's first twenty-four hour satellite-delivered basic cable network, which (first as CBN Cable, then later The Family Channel) grew into a cable giant with seventy-eight million cable subscribers.

In that old church in Brooklyn, God's message was clear: "I want you to claim the airwaves from the prince of the power of the air and give them to the Prince of peace."

Back in the early fall of 1959, as I prayed and fasted, God gave me a portion of His faith. Whether I had a whole "mustard seed" or a part of a "mustard seed," only the Lord can say, but it was enough for the task that He had given me.

When my prayer vigil was completed, the time had come to end my brief sojourn in Brooklyn and I set off to "claim the airwaves." Before I left, I encountered an acquaintance from seminary who asked the customary after-graduation question: "What are you doing now?" Without hesitating, I answered matter-of-factly, "I'm going to Virginia to buy a television station." That statement came out of my mouth as casually as if I had said, "I'm going to the grocery store to buy a loaf of bread." God's faith made something impossible—miraculous—seem as simple as grocery shopping.

I rented a 5x7 U-Haul trailer for our few remaining possessions and hooked it behind the six-year-old used DeSoto automobile that had been given to us by my wife's father. In my pocket, I had a grand total of seventy dollars in cash with which to sustain our family of five while we waited to purchase the Lord's future television station. With hugs and prayers, we said good-bye to our Brooklyn friends and pointed the DeSoto down the streets that would take us across the bridges out of New York City and onto the Jersey Turnpike, then onto Route 13 through the Eastern Shore of Delaware, Maryland, and Virginia, ending with a ferry boat ride across the Chesapeake Bay to the Tidewater cities of which Portsmouth was one.

Looking back, the entire undertaking seemed fraught with peril. I had no job and only a temporary place to stay. I had only enough cash to sustain my family for a few weeks, and certainly no capital to buy a television station. In fact, I had not been in touch with the owner, who had been unavailable for months. I certainly had no oral or written agreement to buy his television station. I was operating in a spiritual realm. Only the Lord could make it happen. I was walking by faith, not sight.

But the Holy Spirit had told me to go. So, empowered with supernatural faith, I packed my family and our meager belongings and went. The laughter and tears, the excitement, and the victories of these early days are too extensive for this book. Just one incident illustrates the supernatural hand of God in the matter.

Between the time that George Lauderdale told me about Channel 27 and my arrival in Portsmouth, Virginia, in mid-November 1959, I had no contact with Tim Bright, the used-car dealer who owned the station. All I had was a price—$37,000—that I believed had been impressed on my mind by the Holy Spirit. I had written Tim to inquire about a sale of the station and its price. Finally, I received an answer: the price for the equipment was $25,000, and the price for the land and the equipment together was $50,000. The number God had given me, $37,000, was right in the middle! In all the documents and agreements that finally came forth, the Lord's number stood. The price was $37,000!

Even though I had no money, I negotiated on the basis of God's promise. On the afternoon of Sunday, October 1, 1961, WYAH-TV began broadcasting on Channel 27. I might add that fifteen minutes before the scheduled airtime, I received the last $5,000 needed to pay off a major creditor and begin broadcasting.

It was a miracle that came about through one and only one thing— the impartation of the supernatural faith that comes from God. God's faith, even as small as a grain of mustard seed, can move mountains.

MIRACLES ARE EFFECTED THROUGH FAITH

This book is about miracles, yet at the heart of every miracle is faith. The apostle Paul, writing to the church in Galatia, gives an eloquent warning against the false teachers who were trying to bring the new Christians into bondage through legalism. These teachers were insisting that the happy, spiritually minded new believers would only perfect their faith in Christ by submitting themselves to the dietary laws, rituals, and commandments of Old Testament Judaism. Here are his words to the Galatian Christians:

Oh, foolish Galatians! What magician has cast an evil spell on you? . . . Did you receive the Holy Spirit by keeping the law? Of course not, for the Holy Spirit came upon you only after you believed the message you heard about Christ. . . . I ask you again, *does God give you the Holy Spirit and work miracles among you* because you obey the law of Moses? Of course not! It is *because you believe* the message you heard about Christ. In the same way, "Abraham believed God, so God declared him righteous *because of his faith.*" (Galatians 3:1–2, 5–6 NLT; emphasis added)

The author of the Book of Hebrews attributes virtually everything of significance in the Old Testament to faith: understanding of the creation of the universe; Abel's acceptance over Cain; Enoch's miraculous transition to heaven; Noah, who by faith built an ark and by his faith condemned the world; Abraham's departure by faith from his home to journey to the promised land; Abraham's sojourn by faith in the promised land; Abraham's willingness by faith to sacrifice his son Isaac; the faith of Isaac, Jacob, and Joseph; Moses, who by faith left the house of Pharaoh to lead Israel; Joshua, who by faith brought down the walls of Jericho; and Rahab, who by faith hid the Israelite spies (11:4–31).

Faith is the biblical key to those heroes who by faith "overthrew kingdoms, ruled with justice, and received what God had promised them. They shut the mouths of lions, quenched the flames of fire, and escaped death by the edge of the sword. Their weakness was turned to strength. They became strong in battle and put whole armies to flight" (vv. 33–34 NLT).

In short, "it is impossible to please God without faith. Anyone who wants to come to him must believe that there is a God and that he rewards those who sincerely seek him (v. 6 NLT).

On the road to miracles, we have seen that faith is essential. Our faith needs to be centered in a mighty Creator God. Jesus told the apostle Peter that he had "little faith" because he let his mind convince him that walking on water was impossible (Matthew 14:31). Jesus refused to give His disciples "increased" faith because a tiny mustard seed of God's faith was more than adequate to perform mighty miracles (Luke 17:5–6).

Yet with all that background, as we explore more fully the recorded ministry of Jesus Christ, we come upon a man—a Roman army officer—who had "great faith" (Matthew 8:10; Luke 7:9). Let's find out why.

THE FAITH OF A ROMAN CENTURION

According to the biblical record, as Jesus was traveling throughout Judea, a Roman centurion (equivalent to a captain in our army having command of one hundred men) approached him. He pleaded, "Lord, my young servant lies in bed, paralyzed and racked with pain."

Jesus said, "I will come and heal him."

Then the officer said, "Lord, I am not worthy to have you come into my home. Just say the word from where you are, and my servant will be healed! I know, because I am under the authority of my superior officers, and I have authority over my soldiers. I only need to say, 'Go' and they go, or 'Come,' and they come. And if I say to my slaves, 'Do this or that,' they do it" (Matthew 8:5–9 NLT).

Jesus was amazed at what He had heard and told the crowd that He had not encountered "such great faith" in all the land of Israel (v. 10). Then Jesus spoke a word of healing, and the servant was healed at that very moment.

Let's dig deeper into this remarkable encounter. This officer represented the most powerful empire on earth. The Roman legions had subjugated every Mediterranean nation. The Roman Empire stood like a giant colossus, spanning territory from the old Babylonian and Assyrian empires, all the way across France and Germany to England. Palestine was merely a minor province of the empire.

Yet here was a seasoned warrior representing mighty Rome, humbling himself before a penniless, itinerant Jewish teacher, even calling him Lord. Imagine what that act entailed. From ancient times until now, conquering armies have despised and humiliated conquered people. Some were killed, some were made slaves, and all were subjugated and demeaned. Although using derogatory terms for people of other nations today is not politically correct, in former days it was. Germans were called "Krauts," Japanese were called "Nips" or "Japs," and North Koreans and North Vietnamese were called "Gooks." What the Japanese did to captured Americans and to the Chinese and South Koreans is too horrible to mention, as is the treatment of captive nations by the Nazis. Rome's armies were certainly no less abusive than those of contemporary history. So it was a matter of great significance when a Roman conqueror, in front of his men, called a Jewish resident of Palestine "Lord." This one who had "great faith" humbled himself.

The Bible tells us, "God resists the proud but gives grace to the humble" (James 4:6; 1 Peter 5:5). In order for anyone to have faith, he or she must be profoundly aware of weakness and inability. One who is self-sufficient will receive nothing from the Lord. Not only does God not cooperate with the proud and arrogant, He actually becomes their enemy. He "resists" the proud. So if you want to experience miracles from God, beware lest you be filled with a sense of your own ability, your own strength, your own wealth, or your own position. God's power comes to those who truly are dead to self but alive to God in Christ (Romans 6:11).

The centurion also had a remarkable ability to equate his sphere of natural authority to Jesus's sphere of spiritual authority. This was the secret of great faith.

The centurion had learned the chain of command. It had been drilled into him, perhaps beaten into him. Roman power flowed from the senate to the emperor, to various consuls, to tribunes, to generals, and then all the way down to individual soldiers through junior officers. When an order was given, it was obeyed instantly. Failure to obey would result in flogging, branding, fine, exile, or even death. So when the centurion received an order, he obeyed. When he gave an order, it was obeyed instantly, because orders down the chain of command carried the authority of the entire Roman Empire.

Day after day during his entire adult life, this Roman officer obeyed orders and gave orders. He, therefore, saw in Jesus a representative of the highest spiritual authority. Of course, Jesus could do in the spiritual realm what the officer did every day in the Roman army: He could carry out orders and give orders.

So he related to Jesus his own experience and humbly indicated an expectation that Jesus had authority to issue orders in the spiritual realm. "Just say the word from where you are, and my servant will be healed!" (Matthew 8:8 NLT).

Clearly, in addition to humility, great faith requires the ability to relate our relevant experiences in the visible world to God's authority in the invisible world. You see, spiritual power and authority are not totally disconnected from our experiences in our everyday life. Faith comes as we are able to make a connection between "I am able to do this" and "Therefore, God must be able to do that."

Somehow this Roman field officer grasped instinctively that after faith, the second most important component needed to effectuate a miracle is *the spoken word.*

Here's how it works. A concept exists in the mind of God, such as healing your body or giving you much-needed funds for an invention, a business, or a charitable organization, or perhaps the raising of someone who is dead. This concept is transmitted from the mind of God to the

Spirit of God. Then it is conveyed from God's Spirit to your spirit and then to your mind. But what happens then? Your mind must speak it forth so the thought, the blessing, the concept, and the miracle become a tangible reality. The centurion grasped this concept. He got it!

Look at what he said to Jesus: "Just say the word from where you are, and my servant will be healed!" Just speak the word! This was the way power was translated into action in the Roman army, and this is the way God translates power into action today. When you read the Genesis story of creation, what do you find over and over again? "Then God said, 'Let there be'" and "it was so." God's spoken command brought forth the wonders of our created universe.

Somehow, without any formal training in the Bible, with no theological education whatsoever, a field officer in the Roman army grasped the motive force of creation. Not works. Not human effort. No exercises in holiness. Merely a simple, commonsense faith that if Jesus Christ pronounced a healing, the healing would take place. "Just say the word."

To this unlettered Roman officer, Jesus Christ paid the highest of compliments: "I have not found such great faith, not even in Israel" (Matthew 8:10).

THE LAME SHALL LEAP WITH JOY

To the casual observer, it would have been easy to conclude that Marlene Klepees was an unfortunate accident of nature. Some might conclude that she had been cursed by God. Certainly, in older days, a less charitable conclusion would be that gross sin in her ancestral line had brought forth a generational curse upon this child. A more loving assessment would have come from the late Dale Evans Rogers, the wife of famous cowboy actor Roy Rogers, who wrote a book boldly announcing that her daughter, who had Down syndrome, was indeed an "angel unaware."

Whatever your conclusion as to the cause of the problem, the simple fact was that Marlene Klepees was born prematurely, weighing only two pounds, with the type of brain damage called *locomotor ataxia*, commonly known as cerebral palsy.

A child or adult with cerebral palsy is unable to send correct signals from the brain to the motor neurons that control speech and the movement of arms and legs. The cerebral-palsied person often speaks with slow, exaggerated facial movements that can result in virtually unintelligible speech and uncoordinated, almost flailing, efforts to move.

A person with cerebral palsy can have a normal, or even genius, level of intelligence. Some are so-called savants, with exceptional artistic or musical skill but low overall IQ. Unfortunately, for the cerebral-palsied person, that intelligent brain cannot make the body that houses it perform on command.

As if premature birth and cerebral palsy weren't enough tragedy for baby Marlene, she suffered a devastating loss at the age of one, when both of her parents were killed in a motorcycle accident. She was raised by great-grandparents and later by foster parents.

Imagine the heartache that each day flooded over this little child. When she tried to form words to speak, her face began a grimace that made each word an ordeal. As other children were running and laughing at play, Marlene was condemned to watch sadly from the sidelines. Try as she would, her legs and arms refused to obey except in spastic jerks. Day after day, hers was the painful realization that there was no way she could throw a ball, skip rope, play hopscotch, or climb the monkey bars at the playground.

Her body refused to function normally, but there was no impairment to Marlene's spirit. When she was twelve years old, some Christian schoolmates took her to a youth rally where she committed her life to the lordship of Christ. The aching void in her heart was filled. She finally found the Father she had longed for all of her life. However, Marlene knew nothing of miracles, so she assumed that she had cerebral palsy because God had made her that way.

For some, the manifestations of cerebral palsy may mitigate with age and physical therapy. Not so with Marlene. In her teenage years, her rebellious muscles not only refused to obey the impulses from her brain, but they began from time to time to spasm violently. In fact, these spasms of her limbs were so violent that they at times broke the bones of the physical therapists who were attending her.

After one extremely violent attack, Marlene was almost paralyzed. There seemed to be no combination of medicine and therapy that could arrest her slide into partial blindness and paralysis.

In December 1980, Marlene was taken from her home in Missouri to the prestigious Mayo Clinic in Rochester, Minnesota. Her former nurse, Nancy White, remembered her condition. "Marlene was a spastic quadriplegic and pretty much dependent on other people to provide for her needs. She needed someone to help her get in and out of bed, in and out of her wheelchair, and to help her go to the bathroom. She really didn't do a lot for herself physically."

Dr. Glen White was Marlene's recreational therapist. He witnessed Marlene's extensive treatment and worsening condition. At that point, she had little control over her head or her neck. Her lips and tongue were swollen, and she drooled. The staff at the clinic didn't have much hope for her ultimate recovery.

Marlene's greatest fear was her impending complete bodily collapse and then being warehoused in a nursing home until death could take her. With all the disappointment, heartache, and pain of her life, she had never given up hope. Now she had hit bottom. Deeply discouraged, she lashed out at the One whom she had known since the age of twelve as a loving Father. "Get out of my life!" she yelled at God. Her heavenly Father understood that this was in truth an anguished cry for help from a child whom He loved.

In that dark night of the soul, Marlene sensed God's warm love and presence all around her. Then God pulled back the curtain and showed this helpless quadriplegic a vision of her future. She saw a church that she had never seen before. She saw specific pictures on the stained-glass windows in the sanctuary. She saw the church doors and the precise detail of the brass door pulls. She saw a minister, wearing a pinstriped suit, who was praying for her. She saw herself riding a bicycle near beautiful green grass, her crippled limbs completely healed. Then she saw a date—March 29—in big, bold letters. She knew it was the date God was going to heal her! March 29 was just three short weeks away.

Marlene reckoned that the promised healing would take place in her home state of Missouri. However, on March 28, she was still in Rochester, Minnesota, and still deteriorating physically.

So she took a step of faith. Her speech was so slurred as to be virtually unintelligible. But with sign language and her slurred guttural speech, she was able to communicate with the attending nurse that she wanted the telephone yellow pages. When the directory was brought to her, she slurred out the word "churches" several times before the nurse opened the book to the page listing all of the Rochester, Minnesota, area churches. With her dim sight, Marlene scanned the pages. Then something wonderful happened. The name of one church began to glow, the letters became bold, and the words *Open Bible Church, Scott Emerson, pastor* almost seemed to be lifted off the page.

Marlene asked her nurse to call that church. When Scott Emerson answered, he thought there was a drunk with severely slurred speech on the line. The caller began asking intriguing questions: Does your church believe in healing? Do you pray for the sick? Have you ever seen a miracle? When Scott finished answering her questions, the seemingly drunken woman said, "Now you can come and see me."

Pastor Scott Emerson was perplexed at this unusual call. Fortunately, there was a nurse on the other end of the line to reassure him that his caller was sincere and in need of help. So he donned his pinstriped suit and drove from the church over to the Mayo Clinic. And how glad he was that he did so, because something was about to happen that would change his life.

When Scott arrived at Marlene's hospital room, he was amazed to hear this severely afflicted, hospitalized young woman give precise details of the church she had never seen, even down to the colors and the location of the pews. What she needed was way beyond his personal experience; nevertheless, he arranged to have her brought to the church on March 29 to be prayed for by a handful of his members who had come for this special purpose.

Pastor Scott Emerson had never seen a miracle take place in his church, but he believed that the God of the Bible still performs miracles today.

Marlene was wheeled into the church sanctuary strapped to her wheelchair, because her body was jerking so wildly with spasms. Her head was lolling from side to side, and she was drooling. She was wearing eyeglasses with very thick lenses. A church member who caught sight of her that night recalled, "I said to myself, 'I didn't realize it was going to be somebody this bad. Lord, this is going to have to be You.'"

So the hour had come, and the sanctuary of the Open Bible Church in Rochester, Minnesota, was the place. Pastor Emerson, who had never seen a miracle in his church, called his members to gather around Marlene's wheelchair and lay hands on her. Then he prayed a simple prayer that God would heal Marlene from the top of her head to the tips of her toes.

When he had finished this simple petition, he leaned down and asked Marlene if she would like to stand up in faith. She nodded yes, and the pastor unbuckled the straps holding her legs to the wheelchair. He lifted both sides of the footrest, and her feet touched the floor. She squirmed and struggled to lift herself into an upright position. She then took a few steps. Each step became stronger. With each step, her pigeon-toed feet became straighter, and then slowly and surely this hopeless, quadric-spastic young woman began to jog around the sanctuary of the church. Almighty God, Marlene's loving heavenly Father, had reached down and kissed His child with His miracle power.

But God did not intend to give her half a miracle. Marlene felt her eyes become warm. When they did, she removed her glasses with the thick lenses and looked around the church with perfect twenty-twenty vision.

As she left the church, Marlene asked to do something that she had been unable to do all of her life—hold and eat an ice cream cone. And who was there at the ice cream parlor? None other than Nancy White, Marlene's dedicated therapist from the Mayo Clinic. "Marlene was one of my wheelchair patients," Nancy relates. "But when I saw her that day, she wasn't in her wheelchair. She was walking, and I couldn't believe it."

Marlene's return to the Mayo Clinic that day caused quite a stir. It had only been two hours since she left, strapped into her wheelchair. She returned to the clinic walking. At that point, the only thing left was for the specialists at the Clinic to discharge Marlene and allow her to return home to Missouri. Today, the hospital records read:

> You returned to the rehabilitation unit that evening walking, something you'd never done since your admission to the unit. And when I saw you back at the clinic some weeks later, you'd improved even more. All signs of previous abnormality were gone. You were able to walk perfectly normal, and your eyesight had improved so much that you did not need to wear spectacles. We were all very thrilled and happy with the outcome of your condition.

The Lame Shall Leap with Joy

After all those tragic years strapped in a wheelchair, Marlene is now living a full and healthy life. She attended Missouri Wesleyan College and for the past eighteen years has traveled extensively to minister to others and to share her amazing story. She owns her own floral shop, where she skillfully arranges flowers with hands that were once practically useless. And she enjoys riding her bike through the countryside, just as she saw in her vision years before.

"I was in a desperate situation, and there was no place else to go but to Jesus Christ with my life—and here I am," she told our *700 Club* producer. "I'm healed. I'm normal. There's nothing that I can't do that everyone else does."

She adds, "I believe this miracle has very little to do with me, and more to do with the Lord. I believe He healed me purposely as a witness to others of what He can and will do."

SMALL STEPS OF FAITH AT THE BEAUTIFUL GATE

Marlene Klepees's heartwarming story seems to come straight out of the pages of the New Testament. In the Book of Acts (3:1–8), we read a story of a beggar who was, like Marlene, lame from birth, and who was carried each day to beg at a place beside the temple gate, the one called the Beautiful Gate. When he saw the apostles Peter and John coming in one afternoon to take part in the three o'clock prayer service, he asked them for some money.

Peter and John said to the lame man, "Look at us." The lame man looked at them, eagerly expecting a gift. Peter then said, "I don't have any money for you. But I'll give you what I have. In the name of Jesus Christ of Nazareth, get up and walk!"

The Bible tells us, "Then Peter took the lame man by the right hand and helped him up. As he did, the man's feet and anklebones were healed and strengthened. He jumped up, stood on his feet, and began to walk! Then, walking, leaping, and praising God, he went into the Temple with them" (vv. 7–8 NLT).

THE FAITH PROCESS THAT LEADS TO MIRACLES

Are there common elements in the miracle experienced by Marlene and the miracle experienced by the beggar at the Beautiful Gate? Yes, there are several important similarities that will give us light on our pathway toward an understanding of miracles and the experience of miracles in our own lives.

Recognize That You Need God's Intervention

First, both of these cases dated from birth, and, from what we can learn, neither case could be helped by human medical intervention. Marlene's problem involved the neural connections between her brain and her muscles. The beggar's condition involved a malformation of the bones and muscles in his feet and ankles. From a human perspective, both cases were hopeless. Both required not just a healing but a creative miracle from God.

Hear and Receive the Word of God

Second, we learn that "faith *comes* by hearing, and hearing by the word of God" (Romans 10:17). Marlene Klepees had come to the point where she had given up faith and asked God to leave her. But at that moment of despair, God spoke to her a clear promise of her healing on March 29. She not only heard the word of God, but she saw a vision from God. On the sure anchor of an unmistakable word, Marlene's faith rose to take the necessary action that prepared the way for her dramatic healing.

The Lame Shall Leap with Joy

There was also a word of God delivered to the lame beggar—not by God Himself, but by a man empowered by Jesus Christ to heal the sick and cast out demons. The word that came from Peter's mouth was energized and made powerful when, on the day of Pentecost, he received the baptism of the Holy Spirit. When Peter commanded, "In the name of Jesus of Nazareth, rise and walk," it was a word of God capable of quickening faith in the crippled man.

My memory fails to recall the thousands of instances in which I have personally given forth an invitation under the power of the Holy Spirit to non-Christians to receive the salvation that is promised to them by the death and resurrection of Jesus Christ. When they hear and receive the word of God, faith arises in their hearts and they are able to turn in faith to a Father who loves them and a Savior who died for them. Of course, the word that brings faith is not just for me or any other minister, but for any Spirit-filled Christian who has been given a divine mandate to speak a word that is energized by the Holy Spirit, capable of bringing faith in those who hear it.

Put Your Faith into Action

Third, we see that faith results in action. The action of a human being arising from faith is not unlike the action of lightning during an electrical storm. As I understand it, the earth is the repository of vast electrical power. At certain times, when a cloud that is electrically charged passes near to earth, a little feeler of electricity leaves the cloud and heads toward the earth. In a split second, it elicits a massive electrical charge from the earth that we say is a bolt of lightning. It appears that the lightning has come from the sky and struck the earth. In truth, the main force of the electrical charge has come from the earth, which has merely responded to the small electrical feeler from the cloud.

So it is with miracles. A word from God brings about faith in our hearts, which in turn leads to a little feeler of action by us toward God. Marlene Klepees put her feet on the floor and struggled to rise from her wheelchair. The lame beggar at the Beautiful Gate took Peter by the hand and stood up. Earlier in Peter's life, when Jesus bade him to walk on the water, Peter got up from his seat, swung his legs over the side of the boat, and then stood on the water.

Those little gestures of faith in action seemed to trigger the miracle response from God. Marlene put her feet on the floor and then struggled to stand. When she did, miracle strength flowed through her body. Suddenly her brain's connection to her limbs was established properly for the first time in her life, and she began not only to walk normally but to run. When the crippled beggar stood up, Luke the physician tells his readers in medical terms that "the man's feet and anklebones were healed and strengthened" (Acts 3:7 NLT). The great miracle came in response to the beggar's action. In like manner, in response to his own act of faith, Peter actually began to walk on water.

When God told me to take seventy dollars and buy a television station, I had to go in faith as far as I was able, and then God gave me the contract, the money, and finally the promised network. In short, my little feeler of faith brought the thunderbolt of God's miracle power.

I believe it is safe to say that if Marlene had not contacted Pastor Emerson, gone to his church for prayer, and then struggled to stand after prayer, there would have been no miracle. She still would have remained desperately cerebral palsied. If the beggar at the Beautiful Gate had not stood on his feet at Peter's command, his feet and anklebones would never have been straightened and strengthened. If Peter had waited for Jesus to throw him out of the boat, he would not have experienced even an incomplete miracle. And if I had stayed in Brooklyn until God dropped $37,000 in my lap, there would not be a Christian Broadcasting Network today—at least not one with me as its founder!

We must wait for God's energized word—whether it is from the Bible, spoken to us directly by the Holy Spirit, or from an angel or a human voice empowered by the Holy Spirit. Then that word will build faith for what is to come. As faith burns in our hearts, we are not being presumptuous when we step out toward the fulfillment of what has been promised—whether it is a miraculous healing, a marriage, a ministry, a business venture, a public office, a role in sports, or the salvation of one or many.

GOD WORKS IN HARMONY WITH HIS PEOPLE

There is a fundamental law in the universe that I call the "law of use," which Jesus described in His parable of the talents. Simply stated, if a person uses well what is given him, he will have more. But if he fails to use what is his, he will lose what little he has. Somehow in the perfect plan of God, there is to be a marriage of what little we do with the great things God does.

I have always been struck by the seeming impertinence of the apostle James, who, as presiding officer of the Jerusalem Council of the early Christian church, made this pronouncement regarding the imposition of Jewish dietary laws on Gentiles who had come to faith in Christ: "It seemed good to the Holy Spirit, *and to us*, to lay upon you no greater burden than these necessary things" (Acts 15:28; emphasis added). I asked myself, "If it seemed good to the Holy Spirit, what possible difference did it make what opinion the early church leaders had? Why add 'to us'?"

Then I began to realize that God works in harmony with His people. Church order depends on our agreeing with the Holy Spirit. Answers to prayer take place when Jesus is in our midst, and we agree on earth concerning what we ask (Matthew 18:19). Upon the prompting of the word of God, we in faith joyously say, "Yes, Lord, we agree with You, and we now step out in faith in accordance with Your word."

Three things must come together from the one seeking a miracle: (1) the word of God, (2) faith arising from the word, and (3) the small steps of faith in accordance with the word. Then God steps in with miraculous power . . . and a miracle bursts forth!

THE WINDS AND THE SEA OBEY HIM

The Sea of Galilee in northern Israel is customarily calm and placid. The surrounding weather is usually balmy and pleasant. But the outwardly tranquil appearance of this big lake belies its extraordinary depth and the violent storms that can roil the surface waters as winds from time to time suddenly sweep down the slopes of the adjoining Golan Heights, which forms its northern border.

The Bible tells us that one day Jesus and His disciples entered a small fishing boat that was docked on the edge of the sea, and then He said to them, "Let us cross over to the other side" (Mark 4:35).

So they set sail. Jesus lay down in the forward part of the boat and, lulled by the gentle lapping of the water against the hull, soon fell asleep. As they approached the middle of the sea where the water was extremely deep, a violent storm arose with waves that towered over the sides of their small vessel. Before long, their boat had begun to fill with water. As it did, the boat sank lower and lower into the sea. The disciples knew they were facing death and in a panic woke up Jesus, who was still sleeping peacefully in the midst of the storm. "Teacher," they shouted, "do You not care that we are perishing?" (v. 38).

With that, Jesus calmly arose and addressed the wind and the waves, much like a pet owner would speak to a big, overexuberant dog. "Peace, be still!" He commanded (v. 39). Suddenly, the wind stopped blowing and the waters were completely placid. The boat and its passengers were safe and unharmed.

A sense of awe came over the disciples of Jesus. They asked, "Who can this be, that even the wind and the sea obey Him!" (v. 41).

TURNING BACK THE STORM

This miracle that took place on the Sea of Galilee became my model in 1961 when I faced an Atlantic storm of far greater intensity than the storm on the Sea of Galilee. Here is what happened.

In November 1959, I had traveled with my family from Brooklyn to Virginia to "claim a television station for the Lord." In January 1960, using two contributions for the required filing fee—one for twenty-five dollars and one for ten dollars, I mailed to the Secretary of State of Virginia an application for a new nonstock, nonprofit corporation to be called the Christian Broadcasting Network, Inc. On January 11, 1960, I received by return mail an official certificate saying that the new corporation was now duly chartered in the State of Virginia.

Through God's grace, I had been able to persuade Tim Bright in the spring of that year to sign over the new corporation title to the land, building, and equipment of his defunct television station, subject to liens from the RCA Corporation and other guarantees of payment.

My new corporation was desperately short of funds. I personally kept the records in a small red ledger book, and during that entire first year of our existence the total revenue was only $8,000. The next year was not much better—$20,000 for an entire year!

I say that to make clear that there were no reserve funds, no fallback position. The slightest shock would have destroyed us. I was walking a tightrope with only God's hand to hold me up.

We now had possession of a television station that was housed in a 70x40 single-story brick building that had been vandalized before I got there. There was one black-and-white television camera that had caught on fire. The lens from the film camera had been ripped off and thrown outside the building. The scrawny trees outside were festooned with old film that the vandals had thrown away. The floors of the offices were covered with papers, and the plate-glass window between the lobby and the tiny studio had been smashed. They had urinated on the floor, and the place reeked of the smell. In short, it was a scene of utter devastation.

Immediately outside the studio, control room, and office building was a self-standing television tower with a heavy UHF antenna set on its top. This area was overgrown with weeds, but it had not been damaged.

The entire complex was located next to a small body of water known as Scott's Creek, which flowed into the Elizabeth River and, in turn, the convergence of the James River, Chesapeake Bay, and the Atlantic Ocean. The entire area was subject to tidal flooding. During one nor'easter, the land around the building was under water that had cascaded over Spratley Street, which ran in front of the station.

I say all of that to emphasize how totally vulnerable I was, how vulnerable the new Christian Broadcasting Network was, and especially how vulnerable our physical plant was.

In those days, the east coast of Virginia and North Carolina was known as "hurricane alley." Hurricanes result as a sort of escape valve for the buildup of heat and moisture at the end of the summer in the Atlantic Ocean off the coast of Africa. The hurricanes form in the Atlantic as swirling tropical storms that follow ocean currents from east to west, where they are steered either into the Caribbean, into Florida, or up the East Coast to the Carolinas or Virginia. Since the eastern part of Virginia juts slightly into the Atlantic, and the Gulf Stream comes close to shore off our coast, this area became a natural landing place for these ocean-born monsters.

One Saturday morning in September 1961, I learned that a Category 4 hurricane, a powerful monster named Esther, was slowly moving up the Atlantic with maximum sustained winds of 144 miles per hour. This huge hurricane was on a track that would bring devastating winds and a storm surge directly into our area. I believed that the television tower for Channel 27 could not withstand a direct hit by a storm with wind gusts exceeding 150 miles per hour. I also believed that if the tower collapsed, it would crush the little studio and the equipment within. With no insurance, no money to rebuild, and no Christian broadcasting . . . it would mark the end of what I knew was God's plan for me. I could certainly have identified with the disciples of Jesus sinking on a stormy sea as they cried out, "Teacher, do You not care that we are perishing?"

In truth, Jesus had told His disciples to "cross over to the other side," not "go out to the middle and drown." And He had told me to claim the airwaves for His glory, not fail in the midst of twisted steel and the rubble of what had once been a television station.

So that Saturday morning, as I stood before the Tidewater Chapter of the Full Gospel Businessman's Fellowship in the ballroom at the top of the Monticello Hotel in downtown Norfolk, I raised my hand toward the massive hurricane out in the Atlantic. Joined by the prayers of the 250 believers in that ballroom, I followed the example of Jesus and spoke to the storm: "In the name of Jesus, I forbid you to come into Tidewater. I command you, in the name of Jesus, to turn around and go back where you came from."

The meeting adjourned a few minutes before noon. When I got into my car, I switched on the car radio and heard a somewhat surprised newscaster deliver this message: "The forward progress of Hurricane Esther has been halted in the Atlantic Ocean. Meteorologists are estimating that a high-pressure ridge out of West Virginia has blocked the storm . . ." I knew better. It was no "high-pressure ridge." It was the hand of God that arrested the giant storm in response to a word of command spoken in the power of the Holy Spirit.

For the next twenty-four hours, the monstrous hurricane rotated slowly out in the ocean and then like a big, dumb beast slowly obeyed and reversed course and began a journey southward.

I have in my possession an Internet version of the storm track of Hurricane Esther. It shows the storm heading directly into Tidewater, Virginia, then turning south and east, then directly south, then due west, far south of our area, then a turn north away from our area, then losing intensity before striking a glancing blow off the coast of New England.

We were safe, and the television station was not touched. The same Jesus who stilled the deadly storm in the Sea of Galilee turned the deadly hurricane away from our shores. Many scoffers laugh at my assertion of what happened, but scoff as they will, they cannot deny the meeting, the prayer, and the permanent record of the storm's track and its remarkable course reversal!

For the past forty-five years or so, God has set an invisible shield around our area, and "hurricane alley" has ceased to be. In fact, it is almost comical to witness these storms' attempts to enter our area. In a contorted maneuver that the local NBC television weatherman dubbed "the Robertson Shuffle," one hurricane tried to enter Tidewater, Virginia, from the south and was forced back to sea. It then went north, turned west, and then turning south, failed again to enter. Once again repulsed, it went back into the ocean and dissipated in the cold water of the North Atlantic.

My experience with these giant storms does not consist of just one victorious experience some forty-five years ago. A number of times during the years I have asked my television audience to join me in prayer to change the course of hurricanes, and, fantastic as it may sound, the Lord has given faith so that the hurricanes have heeded our word.

The message is clear for all of us. Jesus Christ was not just a superhuman God figure who did things that no other human being could ever hope to accomplish. Instead, His life and His teachings and His works of power form a pattern for His people to copy. He said explicitly, "He who believes in Me, the works that I do, he will do also; and greater works than these he will do, because I go to My Father" (John 14:12). Greater works, for every believer! Now! Today! Not just two thousand years ago. Not just for the first hundred years of the church. Your miracles can happen now if you understand what Jesus did and what He taught.

SIX STEPS TO EXPERIENCING GOD'S MIRACLES

We are not the first to wonder how Jesus did what He did. The apostle Peter was with Jesus when a miracle happened; and, of course, being the impetuous one, Peter blurted out a statement which really meant, "That was great, Lord. How did You do it?" The entire story and Jesus's detailed response is found in the eleventh chapter of the Gospel of Mark.

The city of Jerusalem is built on a number of hills that are referred to as mountains: the Mount of Olives, the Temple Mount, Mount Scopus, and so forth. Jesus and His disciples were staying on the back side of the Mount of Olives in a little village known as Bethphage. One morning, they began the brief walk along the crest of the Mount of

Olives on the way to the Temple Mount, which was located down the Mount of Olives, across a ravine known as the Kidron Valley, and then up a modest ascent through the city gate to the Temple Mount from which rose the magnificent holy temple.

On the way, Jesus happened to notice a fig tree in full leaf that held forth the promise of delicious fruit. Since He was hungry, He walked over to the little tree, hoping to pick several figs for His breakfast. Unfortunately, there was not a single fig on the bush; its promise of fruit was an illusion. Jesus looked at the tree and then spoke sharply to it: "May no one ever eat fruit from you again" (v. 14 NIV).

The group then walked down the hill and up to the temple area. What Jesus saw outside the temple both disgusted and angered Him. He shouted at the moneychangers and those selling doves, "Is it not written, 'My house shall be called a house of prayer for all nations'? But you have made it a 'den of thieves'" (v. 17). Then in fury, He fashioned a whip and overturned the tables of the moneychangers and the cages of doves, driving the charlatans out of the temple area.

The symbolism of the fig tree became obvious. The fig tree is a symbol of Israel (Hosea 9:10). Its leaves promised fruit, but there was none. The gorgeous gold-encrusted temple with its splendidly clad priests and elaborate rituals held out the promise to the hungry-hearted supplicant that here, they might encounter Almighty God. Instead of God, they found the tables of mendacious commerce. When Jesus cursed the fig tree, the meaning clearly transcended a little tree with no fruit—He was, in effect, cursing the religious system of an entire nation that was producing rotten fruit.

The next day, when Jesus and His disciples were returning to the temple, they once again passed by the fig tree, which was completely withered right down to the roots. Peter stared in amazement and said, "Rabbi, look!

The fig tree which You cursed has withered away" (Mark 11:21). Since what he had observed was obvious, we must conclude that his exclamation contained the question, "How did You do it?" It was to this implied question that Jesus set forth six steps to experiencing God's miracles:

Step 1: Have Faith in God
The first step in being part of a miracle is to have faith in God. You might refer back to chapter 1 to reread the high points of what this means.

Step 2: Speak a Command
Second, in the presence of God, filled with the word of God, and having the faith of God, speak a command. Speak to the mountain, speak to the storm, speak to the fig tree, speak to the disease, speak to the finances, and speak to the demons. In the presence of God, you see what He is doing; you learn His word; and then, as His representative on earth, you speak the command just as Jesus did.

Without question, the concept of speaking something into existence, although absolutely biblical, is foreign to most Christians. Without denigrating the faith or spiritual commitment of any person who lives in a hurricane zone, I share with you the following story.

In the mid-1970s, my wife, Dede, who was thoroughly familiar with how we dealt with hurricanes, traveled with our friend, Nora Lam, and a tour group on a missionary journey and evangelistic crusade to the island nation of Taiwan. The group visited the capital city of Taipei without incident and then journeyed to the large industrial port of Kaohsiung. While they were there, an Asian version of a hurricane (called a "typhoon") arose in the Pacific Ocean and began bearing down rapidly on Taiwan. Its apparent target was Kaohsiung.

Each morning, the group gathered for prayer. These prayer meetings were conducted in turn by one of the clergymen traveling with the group. Sensing the urgency of the situation, my wife approached the clergy leader for that day and said, "There is a big typhoon heading right at us. We have to command it to go away."

"Of course we will pray about it," was the reply.

"No, not just pray about it," my wife insisted. "We must rebuke it and command it to go away."

"You want me to command a typhoon?" came the startled reply.

"That's exactly what I want," Dede insisted. "Do it now."

So the good man of the cloth bravely faced the group with the news of the typhoon's impending arrival and said, "Mrs. Robertson says that we should command the storm in Jesus's name to turn away." So he closed his eyes and with as much faith as he was able to muster said, "I rebuke you, typhoon. In the name of Jesus Christ of Nazareth, I command you to turn back and spare this island."

To his surprise, in a short time the typhoon reversed course and went away from Taiwan. But somehow the storm sensed a lack of real faith among the people, and after it had gone several hundred miles out into the ocean, it turned around with fury and headed back to the city where these American Christians were staying.

The next morning, my wife approached the next clergyman who was the designated prayer leader. "Brother," she said, "a terrible typhoon is heading our way."

"Yes," he replied. "We will pray about it."

By now, Dede did not think that it was the task of a woman to instruct every clergyman on the tour how to pray away storms, so she sat down and let the second clergyman do it his way. This is how he prayed: "O Lord, a great and terrible storm is heading our way. Please don't let it harm us. Amen!"

Obviously, a prayer like that doesn't stop much of anything. In a few hours, this monstrous storm engulfed Kaohsiung and did almost a billion dollars' worth of damage. It smashed the windows out of the fourth-floor room where Dede was staying, and water flooded into the room. Fortunately, she had sufficient foresight to place her luggage and clothes on the shelf in the closet, so the water didn't harm them.

Now the little group was thoroughly miserable. Their crusade was temporarily canceled. There was no electricity, inadequate food, no drinking water, and soggy living accommodations. But sure enough, in answer to the pastor's prayer, none of them was injured by the storm.

I was amused when Dede came back and told me very sincerely, "You know, I was so disappointed. Those people just didn't have any faith!" The truth was they had plenty of faith, but they just didn't know how to use it. As we study what Jesus did, we will learn about faith for miracles.

Step 3: Be Specific

To the wind and the sea, Jesus spoke only three words: "Peace, be still." To the fig tree, He forbade any further fruitfulness. To the mountain, His command was clear: "Be removed and cast into the sea!" To a demon, He said, "Be quiet and come out of him"; to a dead girl, He said, "Little girl arise"; and to his friend Lazarus, whose body was in the grave and decomposing, His command was simply, "Lazarus, come forth!"

Jesus said, "My Father has been working until now, and I have been working" (John 5:17). He saw what the Father was doing and He heard what the Father was saying, then He did what the Father was doing and He said what the Father was saying. Although Jesus did seek His Father's will in prayer (Matthew 6:10; 26:42), never, ever did He nullify a specific faith command by the faith killer that contemporary Christians think makes them sound spiritual: "If it be Thy will."

Imagine a boat sinking in a violent storm and a command of faith, "Peace, be still . . . if it is God's will." Imagine saying to a little dead girl, "Arise, if it is God's will." If it isn't God's will, then don't command it.

Step 4: Do Not Doubt

And if it is God's will, don't negate the powerful word by a phrase reflecting doubt. King David wrote in the Psalms, "My heart is steadfast, O God" (57:7). James, the half brother of the Lord, wrote, "If any of you lacks wisdom, he should ask God. . . . But when he asks, he must believe and not doubt, because he who doubts is like a wave of the sea, blown and tossed by the wind. That man should not think he will receive anything from the Lord; he is a double-minded man, unstable in all he does" (1:5–8 NIV).

Here is the principle: if two on earth agree, it will be done for them (Matthew 18:19). In the realm of miracles, the agreement is between the Spirit of God and your human spirit. The inspiration comes from the Holy Spirit of God, who is showing His will for a miracle to come forth. It is God who wanted to raise Lazarus from the dead. It is God who wanted to heal Marlene Klepees. It is God who wanted to bring CBN into being. It is God who wanted to rescue our fledgling ministry from the power of a killer hurricane.

It is always God prompting, leading, encouraging, challenging . . . setting before us goals that seem impossible. It is God who opens for us wonderful worlds of opportunity. It is God who prompts us to extend His kingdom and shows us how to care for the downtrodden and needy.

What God wants is for us to agree with Him on earth for the blessings He desires to give us. That means our spirits and our emotions must be in agreement with His Spirit. When that agreement takes place, our speech becomes His speech, and we become surrogates for God on earth. Then, if we don't doubt—if we don't disagree with God—if we are not constantly allowing the rationalism of our minds to convince us that miracles are not possible—if we are not double-minded—then, according to Jesus, we will have the things that we say!

Step 5: Appropriate the Answer Immediately

Jesus said, "Whatever things you ask when you pray, believe that you received them, and you will have them" (Mark 11:24). It is said that the vast majority of Christian people who pray in the morning cannot recall by afternoon what they prayed for only a few hours before. Miracle prayer reaches into the invisible world and knows precisely that an answer has come—not will come, but *has come* . . . now. It is yours when you pray, not at some distant moment in the future.

Imagine for a moment the following: Suppose you are destitute and have a critical need for one hundred dollars. Suppose you come to me and say, "I am desperate. I have no food. My electricity and water are being cut off. I must have a hundred dollars now. Will you give it to me?" At that moment of your request, I immediately reach into my pocket, take out a one-hundred-dollar bill, and hold it out to you. But you are so absorbed with your problems and your prayer that you beg again. "Please, please help me. I only want a hundred dollars. Please hear me!"

Again, I hold out to you the money, but you ignore it and beg even more earnestly. "Please, I am starving. I have to have money to buy food." Once again, I hold out the money, but once again you are absorbed with your problem, doubtful that I am willing to help you. Finally, you lose all hope and walk away sadly, concluding that I care nothing about your problem and am merely ignoring you.

Now think of the same situation, but with a different dynamic. As you ask for help, you expect an answer, and when the money is extended, you reach out and take it, throw your arms around me in gratitude, and then march off happily to the grocery store to purchase your supplies.

Remember that when you pray, a loving, all-powerful God hears your prayer and sends out an answer immediately to coincide with His perfect timing for your life. So when you pray, appropriate the answer and thank Him for it. But don't try to force God's hand. The visible answer will come in His perfect time. As with Marlene, it will be your March 29 when your promised miracle takes place. While you are waiting, don't try to impose your faith on others by incurring debts that you do not have money to pay off merely because you are "trusting the Lord for a miracle," and do not write checks on bank accounts that do not have enough money to cover them.

Step 6: Forgive Those Who Have Wronged You

Jesus put it this way: "When you stand praying, if you hold anything against anyone, forgive him, so that your Father in heaven may forgive you your sins" (Mark 11:25 NIV).

For miracles to occur, there must be communication between you and God. You have to sense His presence, to feel in your spirit the limitless potential of the invisible world, where all things are possible. In essence, you must be sufficiently in tune with the Holy Spirit that it seems you are seeing the kingdom of God. This is precisely what Jesus told a Jewish elder named Nicodemus, who had come seeking a revelation about heaven. Jesus told this spiritual and political leader a truth many of us take for granted: "Unless one is born again, he cannot see the kingdom of God" (John 3:3).

When God first created man on earth, that man, Adam, enjoyed a clear, unobstructed view of God and the spiritual realm. Adam's spirit was an unbroken reflector upon which the light of God could shine perfectly.

But when Adam sinned and was subsequently driven from paradise and access to the tree of life, his view of God was forever murky. What the theologians call the *imago dei*, the image of God, was forever shattered. Never again could Adam grasp the full spiritual reality of the life with God in paradise. Instead, his lot was blood, sweat, tears, and eventual physical death. He came from dust, and he would return to dust (Genesis 3:19).

But Jesus gave us the opportunity to have the inner reflector in our spirit made like new. We could, by faith in Him, be "born again" and, in turn, once more be given sight into the kingdom of heaven. That sight is crucial to miracle power, and that sight depends on our sins being continually forgiven and washed away.

Jesus teaches that if you refuse to forgive people who have hurt you—who have cheated you, lied about you, molested you, raped you, or abandoned you—then you will lose the forgiveness, or at least the consciousness of forgiveness, of your sins. Without that forgiveness, there will be no more sight into the heavenly realm and, consequently, no faith and no miracles. Forgiving others is not an optional extra, but the heart of the matter.

Regardless of the facts that you may feel support your bitterness toward another person, regardless of how justified your side of the argument may be, you must forgive or you will lose out on miracle power. "When you stand praying, if you hold anything against anyone, forgive him, so that your Father in heaven may forgive you your sins" (Mark 11:25 NIV). These are not my instructions, but the clear commandment of the Son of God.

The Winds and the Sea Obey Him

My dear friend, the late Demos Shakarian, told me a wonderful story that illustrates this great truth. Demos's grandfather came with his son, Isaac, from Armenia to America because of the revelation of God to a young Russian boy, who warned the Armenian Christians of the terrible massacres that the Turks were going to perpetrate upon them. This teenager had a series of dreams and visions that resulted in not only a warning to the Armenians to flee their homeland, but a detailed map showing a journey to America with California as the final destination.

Most of the villagers refused to move from their established homes and occupations because of the warning of a teenage boy. But Demos's grandfather believed the warning, sold his property, and took his wife and son by ship to New York, then traveled on to California. The Shakarian family arrived in Los Angeles near the turn of the century and were delighted to find people who were worshiping God at the Azusa Street revival as they did in the old country. The family began to eke out a living as farmers, selling milk and produce from a pushcart in Los Angeles. Land was cheap in Downey, California, and little by little, Isaac Shakarian saved his money and began buying the land for a farm and a dairy herd. As Los Angeles grew, the Shakarian family prospered until they owned and operated what was said to be the third-largest dairy farm in the United States.

When Isaac Shakarian died, his large estate was not in good shape because of debt, taxes, and poor estate planning. However, Isaac had a good friend and adviser whom Isaac's heirs, including his son Demos, were counting on to help in this crisis. To their surprise, however, their trusted family friend decided to profit from their misfortune and seized large portions of Isaac's estate.

Demos was hurt, then angry. And then he began to hate this man who had abused the trust of his deceased father, Isaac. As the hatred grew, Demos lost all joy. He had no spiritual power. He no longer had the sweet fellowship he had known for so many years with the Lord. He was empty and floundering.

Then God gave Demos a clear yet painful course of action. He was to call the man who had betrayed him and arrange a meeting. The time and place of the meeting was set. At the appointed time, the man was driven to meet Demos at the appointed place in a black stretch limousine.

Demos opened the back door of the limousine and stepped inside. A look of terror showed on the man's face. Was there to be a beating— a killing—a shouting match—a lawsuit? The man could not hide his guilt, and now the day of reckoning had arrived. However, what happened next astounded him.

In a calm and loving voice, Demos explained that he had hated him for what he had done to the family. Then he said simply, "Will you please forgive me for hating you?"

At that, the man broke down and cried. He apologized for his behavior and asked for Demos's forgiveness. They forgave each other and hugged one another. When Demos stepped out of that limousine, the bitterness was gone, the anger was gone, the peace of God was flooding his being, and God's presence returned in power.

Soon after he returned to his office, his telephone rang. On the other end was the real-estate manager of a department store chain that had built a large store on a heavily traveled piece of land that they had leased from Demos some years ago. They had decided to give up the site but wanted to fight over who would own the building.

Demos heard the caller saying, "Demos, rather than fight over ownership of the store on your land, we have decided just to give it over to you free and clear, at no charge!"

It had taken the Lord only a few hours after His servant surrendered his bitterness to give him a huge financial blessing, which, it is my impression, may have been worth more than the portion of Isaac's estate that had been taken from him. It was a true miracle!

God is true to His word. If you want to see miracles in your life, remember, "When you stand praying, if you hold anything against anyone, forgive."

A NEW CREATION

The apostle Paul wrote to the church at Corinth in ancient Greece, "If anyone *is* in Christ, *he is* a new creation; old things have passed away; behold, all things have become new" (2 Corinthians 5:17). A new mind, a new soul, a new spirit, a new person . . . what greater miracle can there be than this?

Why do we need to become a "new creation"? If we go back to the beginning, we learn that the first couple, Adam and Eve, lived directly in God's presence. Adam and Eve were created to do good, not evil. They were free to express themselves in any way they saw fit and to enjoy any pleasure that came their way. Whatever they did was open, spontaneous, and full of childlike joy. They reveled in the green grass, the fragrant flowers, the warm blue sky, the crystal-clear waters, the endless varieties of delicious fruit—so delicious, as philosopher and author C. S. Lewis put it in *The Great Divorce*, that "men on earth today would kill for just one taste of it." They delighted in the companionship of the tame and friendly animals and could undoubtedly communicate with them with no difficulty.

Since they were husband and wife, Adam and Eve were free to

express their love and affection for one another as they saw fit. Human sexuality was natural, normal, a gift of God. They were innocent, naked, unashamed, unafraid, filled with the love of God, love for one another, love of the animals, and love of what they were learning of God's wonderful creation. This was paradise . . . the paradise that a good God intended for the creatures made in His image, to whom the entire planet Earth had been given as their kingdom to care for and rule over.

In order for Adam and Eve to learn the difference between good and evil, God placed in paradise one special fruit tree. He then told Adam and Eve to enjoy everything that was there as they saw fit, but there was the fruit of one tree that He did not want them to eat. So day after day, as they passed by that tree, they could say to themselves, "God does not want us to eat the fruit of that tree. Not eating from it is the will of God, so that is good. Eating from it is contrary to the will of God, so that is evil. Everything else we feel like doing is good, because God made us this way."

Day after day, they reveled in the garden of delights, where there was no sickness, no pain, no death, no tears, and no sorrow; where their bodies remained youthful, muscular, and vigorous, without cancer, heart disease, high blood pressure, diabetes, Parkinson's, Alzheimer's, lupus, malaria, influenza, or any of the other terrible diseases that plague humanity today. As they daily enjoyed guilt-free pleasures that only the Creator could conceive for them, they were gradually being schooled in righteousness.

We are told that it takes twenty-one days, on average, for a person to form a habit or to break a habit. At creation, Adam and Eve were in moral neutral, with a strong pull toward God. The theologians use a term to describe this condition—*posse non peccare*, able not to sin. After twenty-one days, the habit of choosing good over evil would have become so ingrained in Adam and Eve that they would have become *non posse peccare*, not able to sin. When they reached that state of perfection, we can only begin to imagine the heights of wisdom and power God would have given them. Slowly but surely, He would have entrusted to them the secrets of His universe—marvels of space and time that we can only dream about today.

But it was not to be. Adam and Eve were enticed by a malevolent being that placed doubt in their minds about the goodness of God. The same lie in the Garden of Eden is the lie of the devil today: "God is keeping something good from you because He knows that when you drink it, smoke it, inject it, chew it, or do it, you will be transported in ecstasy and be like God." That lie cost the human race paradise. Today, it is costing tens of millions of people their health, their happiness, their families . . . and their very lives.

From paradise, the human race rapidly descended into moral chaos. They turned from God and began worshiping statues made in their own image and then in the image of animals, birds, and reptiles. Their inner beings became darkened. They reveled in sexual perversions, and God gave them over to a depraved mind.

Consider how far the human race had fallen in a few thousand years from paradise to the debauchery of the Roman Empire. The apostle Paul wrote to first-century Christians who lived in the capital of the Roman Empire, "They have become filled with every kind of wickedness, evil, greed and depravity. They are full of envy, murder, strife, deceit and malice. They are gossips, slanderers, God-haters, insolent, arrogant and boastful; they invent ways of doing evil; they disobey their parents; they are senseless, faithless, heartless, ruthless. Although they know God's righteous decree that those who do such things deserve death, they not only continue to do these very things but also approve of those who practice them" (Romans 1:29–32 NIV).

GOD'S PLAN TO REDEEM HIS PEOPLE

Yet God had a plan then and a plan now to redeem the race and to give people trapped by evil desires a way out.

In 593 BC, the prophet Ezekiel, writing under the inspiration of the Holy Spirit, outlined God's future plan for His covenant people, Israel: "I will sprinkle clean water on you, and you will be clean; I will cleanse you from all your impurities and from all your idols. I will give you a new heart and put a new spirit in you; I will remove from you your heart of stone and give you a heart of flesh. And I will put my Spirit in you and move you to follow my decrees and be careful to keep my laws" (36:25–27 NIV).

God had not abandoned the human race. His future plan is to destroy the present material universe and create a new heaven and a new earth. But for now, He sent to earth a second Adam, who would live without sin and be the perfect human being that the Creator intended to bring forth at the beginning. Then, as the representative of the entire human race, this perfect second Adam would take upon Himself all of the sin, the evil, the cruelty, and the degradation that the entire human race experienced throughout history.

As our representative, Jesus Christ, the second Adam, experienced a horrible death and, at that moment, tasted the infinite spiritual agony of separation forever from the Father. Then God declared, "My justice has been served; now My love will triumph."

One by one, by tens, by hundreds, by thousands, by millions, people who believe in the death and resurrection of Jesus and who make Him Lord of their lives will become part of a new creation—a new human race. They will be given a transformed spirit. Then God will place His Spirit within them to enable them to keep His laws. He will cleanse them from their previous sins and adopt them as His sons and daughters. These people will form the company of the redeemed who will be the residents for all eternity of the new heaven and the new earth that God is planning to create. Although they are not totally free from the pulls and urges of their human natures, day by day they are being given by God the power to put to death their old nature, to resist the temptations of the devil, and to live victoriously as new creatures in Christ (2 Corinthians 4:16).

Some transformations are more dramatic than others. Here is one of them.

ALIVE FOR THE FIRST TIME

Annie Arthur grew up afraid. We don't know what trauma scarred her life as a child. Was she dropped or injured at birth? Was she sexually molested? Was she beaten? Was she constantly battered by verbal abuse? Was she exposed to the occult? Was there an accident or terrible death in the family? These are the things that can twist the souls of little children and remain to haunt them as adults. In Annie's case, we don't know what happened, but her fears were real. "I don't ever remember a day waking up without being afraid in my heart."

As she grew into an adult, her fears grew with her. Annie became a prisoner of her own thoughts. She says, "If I could just keep myself in a house, locked up, and nobody to come near me, that's how I was. I would sit at the table for hours, smoking and drinking coffee, and wonder why I was ever born; I thought fear was placed in me at birth."

Like millions of others trying to escape the scars of childhood, Annie tried taking pain pills as a way out. Soon she had traded her fears for an addiction. "Over a couple of years, I started out at three pills a day," she says. "Then it grew to six, nine, ten pills first thing in the morning, and ten more about four o'clock in the afternoon. So by the end of the addiction, I was taking about twenty to thirty pills a day. Then I would couple it with alcohol. Anything to keep shoving that . . . whatever was rising in me . . . down."

Annie became so despondent that she tried to end her life. "That was the thought going through me," she says. "Just end your life; you'll never amount to anything; you're so afraid of everything."

Her suicide attempt failed, and she was hospitalized. Her abused brain rebelled and sent her into convulsions—grand mal seizures. Annie's life was a picture of despair. But Annie was not just hurting herself; she was also hurting her husband and daughter.

How many troubled young people flee into marriage in the hope of escaping the trauma of their childhood? And how few prospective spouses see that the cute cheerleader or the popular athlete has been deeply scarred psychologically by some abuse that may be hidden in his or her subconscious? After the early romance and the storybook wedding comes the dreadful unveiling when that damaged inner self begins to assert itself more and more, and the marriage seems no longer to be made in heaven but becomes hell on earth.

When Bob Arthur appeared in her life, Annie had hoped for love, the kind of love that would overcome her lifelong fears. Bob was unable to read into the recesses of Annie's soul. All he knew was that she appeared to be a lovely girl with whom he could spend the rest of his life.

Annie, on the other hand, did not realize that her Prince Charming was not the rock of stability for which she had longed but a troubled and insecure man, given to outbursts of rage, with a deep spiritual emptiness inside him that even the most perfect wife could not fill. Psychologists speak of "codependency." In this marriage, the wife was despairing of ever being released from the grip of fear and needing love, safety, and reassurance; the husband had emotional problems and an empty life, in need of someone to fill a massive void.

All the love Bob and Annie had hoped to find in each other was gone. According to Bob, "It was a day-to-day life; it wasn't a marriage, but just watching after her. Every time I left for work, I didn't know if she'd be there when I got back—if my daughter would be there. She had ransacked the house at times, so you didn't know what would happen."

From Annie's point of view, "I just couldn't live like him, and it was warfare. It was definite heaven and hell raging for control of my house." She continued, "After our daughter was born, he had an outburst of anger and destroyed my whole house, literally."

Bob knew something had to be done. "There were even times in the bar," he recalls, "when I said this is going to get old one day, and what is it going to take next time to fill this void? Because nothing ever kept it filled . . . just momentarily."

Two human beings gripped with fear, rage, despair, emptiness . . . locked into a loveless marriage where each one feared the next provocation, the next violent outbreak from the other. Annie felt the only way out was suicide.

Bob, however, turned to the church, where he gave his life over to the Lord Jesus Christ. "I knew Jesus Christ was the only way, beyond any shadow of a doubt," he says. "Immediately, I quit smoking, drinking, swearing, hanging out with the friends I had . . . God just completely turned my whole life around."

Bob found what he was looking for; the aching void in his life was now filled. But Bob's transformed life was too much for Annie to deal with. Her reaction was almost humorous. She recalls, "Now I was living with this holy man, and it was very difficult, because he was so righteous and I wasn't. I mean, we were so different."

Annie resented Bob's relationship with the Lord, and their home became a war zone. Annie remembers, "When I knew it was the night Bob would go to evangelism class, I'd start drinking the minute he got home from work, so he could watch me drinking my little beers while I was cooking dinner. That way, he'd be sure to know I'd be drunk when he got home after class."

But Bob's conversion was real. He really was a "new creation" in Christ. With amazing candor, he says, "Over a four-year period, God put His love in me so much that I couldn't get mad at her. She would do things, and she would get mad at me just because I wasn't mad at her. But I couldn't get mad at her, no matter what she did."

And the things that Annie did to incite Bob's rage would test the ingenuity of a Hollywood scriptwriter trying to sketch the plot of a show about a dysfunctional family. "I would smoke one cigarette after the other, and blow it in his direction, and just constantly do things to harass him, waiting, just hoping he'd give up on me. I could feel something going on in the house. There was a war raging without words from him. But I was a raving maniac most of the time, because he wouldn't fight with me no matter what I did. He wouldn't argue with me or fight with me. He would just gracefully leave the room or leave the situation."

Bob, on the other hand, had no intention of giving up on his wife. "I just felt for her," he says, "and I realized it was simply spiritual warfare, so I would pray for her, anoint her at night, and say things that were not as though they were." Bob never stopped praying for Annie. He persevered in faith, all the while expecting a miracle. Then it happened! Here is Annie's amazing testimony:

> I flew into the house, and the minute I saw Bob, I said, "I can't stand living with you anymore," and I ran to my bedroom and threw myself on my bed.

He came over by the bed and knelt down and said very cautiously, "Annie, you know we can pray about this." He was very careful about God things. But in my mind, I just said, "God, get him out of my face!" Then Ann [my daughter] started crying in her room, and Bob said, "I'll be right back." While he was gone, I jumped off the bed and went into the bathroom.

I fell on the floor and I just started crying. I said, "God, I have nothing to offer You. I'm just so afraid." And God said, "If you'll give Me your heart, I'll make it new." He said, "My peace will be your peace." So I just asked Him to come into my life at that moment.

When Annie came out of the bathroom, she was transformed. According to her husband, Bob, "She didn't say a word, but I knew it. She walked out of the bathroom, and she was alive! She'd been dead for so many years, so empty, so void of everything."

Annie was a new creation. Formerly, her spirit had been killed by overwhelming fear. Now she was renewed on the inside by "joy unspeakable and full of glory" (1 Peter 1:8 KJV). She says, "The more I fell in love with God through the Word, because the Bible says that perfect love casts out all fear [1 John 4:18], the more I found that I wasn't afraid. God has so restored all the years the enemy has robbed in my life."

A new creation, a new birth, unspeakable joy, the peace of God, the blessed hope of eternal life, the leading of the Spirit, close fellowship with the Creator. Troubled, rebellious, fearful, suicidal Annie got all this and more when she turned her life over to Jesus. Her words have become a mighty shout of joy: "I just feel alive for the first time in my life. I feel really happy to wake up in the morning, where there was a time I couldn't stand to wake up. I would beg God to take me in my sleep so I wouldn't have to see the morning sun. Today, every day is a new day!"

One of the great tragedies in human history springs from the role played by fruits and plants in the lives of people. At creation, the human race was given dominion over the animals, the birds, the reptiles, and the fruit trees and seed-bearing plants. Mankind was to cultivate fruit trees, seed-bearing plants, and herbs. These plants existed to feed people and their livestock, and to provide medicine and fragrances and certain types of shelter.

But over the years, the role has been reversed. Instead of masters of the vegetable kingdom, human beings made in the image of God are now the slaves of the products of fruit, plants, and vegetables. Jesus Christ came to set them free from this unnatural bondage.

In the United States of America, the best estimates available to me indicate more than sixteen million Americans are slaves to fermented corn, barley, hops, and grapes; nearly three million Americans are slaves to a powder taken from the cocoa plant; over six hundred thousand Americans are slaves to crushed and distilled seeds of the opium poppy; miscellaneous others are slaves to the fermented juice of apples, peaches, and apricots; and at least fifteen million are slaves to the seeds of the cannabis plant known by its Spanish name, which means "Mary Jane," or marijuana.

These slaves often hate what their masters force them to do. They see their health deteriorating. They see their finances evaporating. They see their families shattered. They see their minds dulled and their physical strength vanishing. Cry out as they will, relief is seldom in sight. But to some of the slaves, a Champion appears who breaks their chains and sets them free.

A New Creation

James Herring was one whose release from alcoholism can only be termed miraculous. Herring's slavery to alcohol was so intense that not one of four separate extended stays in rehabilitation centers could break it.

When an alcoholic tries to rid his system of the alcohol, each time is painful. Withdrawal can be a hellish nightmare, complete with agonizing cramps, vomiting, shaking and sweating, mucus pouring from the nostrils, and a mind full of terrifying images brought on by what is called delirium tremens, commonly known as the "d.t.'s." The polite term used to describe the ghastly experience that rids the system of the poison of alcohol is called detoxification, or detox, the process of allowing the body to eliminate the alcohol toxins.

In detox, there is no attempt at counseling or rehabilitation. Instead, the alcoholic is confined in an area where it will be impossible to obtain more of the poison his body so desperately craves. The weeklong agony of withdrawal is allowed to run its painful course. Six times, in a desperate attempt to free himself from the slavery of alcohol, James Herring submitted to detoxification, and six times his master from the vegetable world reached out and took him back.

James Herring's struggle echoes the cry of the apostle Paul in the seventh chapter of the Book of Romans: "When I want to do good, evil is right there with me. For in my inner being I delight in God's law; but I see another law at work in the members of my body, waging war against the law of my mind and making me a prisoner of the law of sin at work within my members. What a wretched man I am! Who will rescue me from this body of death?" (vv. 21–24 NIV).

As Herring describes his slavery to booze, "It had complete control of me. It was my life. It took over everything. Nothing else mattered—nothing."

That is the testimony of millions of men and women enslaved to alcohol, narcotics, and the chemical creations of illegal laboratories. Nothing else matters. They will sell their possessions, their futures, their children, even their own bodies for one more "fix" to ease the craving that their slave masters have created within them. One of the most revolting accounts I ever heard came from the lips of a reformed alcoholic who testified that he stole the shoes off the feet of the body of his little girl as she lay in a casket in a funeral home in order to get enough money to buy one more drink at a nearby tavern.

The apostle Paul asked, "Who will rescue me from this body of death?" There is One who alone can save us from our own bodies.

James Herring finally found Him. "One night I was lying there in the middle of the night. I had run out of alcohol. I was getting sick with the shakes. It hurt all over. I turned on the TV, and I hit Play on the VCR. Where it came from, I have no idea because I didn't tape it."

In his painful stupor, James began watching a religious television program that had mysteriously appeared on the tape in his VCR—the *700 Club*. He watched the full hour of the program and then did something he had never done before. In the middle of the night, shaking and aching from withdrawal, this confirmed alcoholic began to pray with the host of the television program.

As he tells it, "I prayed with Gordon to receive Christ, and then I realized that, while I was watching it, I wasn't feeling as bad. It took my mind off how I felt, so I rewound it and played it again. And I watched it again. I started praying every morning, and the next thing that happened was that I started drinking less. I started going longer periods of time without drinks."

James was encouraged by the *700 Club* program to read the Bible and go to church. After twenty years of slavery to alcohol, the power of the Lord Jesus Christ did what no amount of psychological rehabilitation could do. James is free. He is sober. He is under the loving lordship of Jesus in control of his own life. Free at last!

In the words of the apostle Paul, "Who will rescue me from this body of death? Thanks be to God—through Jesus Christ our Lord. . . . Therefore, there is now no condemnation for those who are in Christ Jesus, because through Christ Jesus the law of the Spirit of life set me free from the law of sin and death" (Romans 7:24–25; 8:1–2 NIV).

A SECOND CHANCE

Addiction not only causes grief and tragedy in a life, but it can devastate children as well. Janet Taylor's childhood in North Carolina was far from ideal. Janet's mother died when she was five, after which she went to live with her grandmother, a hardworking woman whom Janet described as "the best cook this side of the Mississippi."

Janet affectionately called her "Big Mama." Big Mama did her best to care for her granddaughter, but when she died, Janet, scared and lonely, got passed around among her poor relatives. She thought that she could make a better life for herself by striking out on her own. So in her late teens, Janet joined the United States Navy.

Instead of freedom and a new and better life, this is when her bondage began. In the navy, Janet fell in with a wild crowd and started smoking marijuana. Then she moved to something harder—cocaine.

She recalls, "I got strung out on cocaine while I was in the navy. It was just accepted where I was, you know, as a matter of fact . . . that you were cool if you were using some form of drugs. So I got in with that crowd."

Narcotics numb the senses and the keen sense of right and wrong. Along with the cocaine came a brief sexual relationship with a sailor that led to a pregnancy and then the birth of a baby boy. Janet took her newborn son to the home of the sailor's parents in Daytona, Florida.

Although the parents were willing to put up with their son's unwed girl-friend and her out-of-wedlock child, they had no intention of having a reg-ular cocaine user living in their home. We can only guess how many shouting matches went on in that house. Janet's only comment was, "We didn't get along well. I was on drugs and they knew it, so they put me out."

Now began the cruel price of addiction. Janet was in her early twen-ties, with little education, no job, no house to live in, and a baby to support. In America, the fastest-growing and most pitiful segment of poverty is made up of single women with children. Janet Taylor was fast becoming a statistic of hopelessness.

Somehow she was able to talk her baby's grandparents into caring for him. She, in turn, hit the streets to sell her body to lustful strangers to get the money to sustain herself and her growing drug habit.

She was damaged goods—a strung-out prostitute longing for some-one to take care of her. Her choice of caregiver was tragically unwise. Not only did the man she hooked up with get her pregnant with a sec-ond child, but he beat her until she agreed to prostitute for him.

She wandered the streets—tired, lonely, and heartsick—while offering her body time and time again for the money to pay her boyfriend pimp and to pay the demands of her cocaine master. As she walked the streets, Janet was arrested for prostitution more times than she could recall. Desperate to get off the streets, she escaped a prison sentence by promis-ing the judge that she would leave Florida and go back to North Carolina.

She wanted freedom, but her cruel taskmaster was reluctant to let her go. Once she was in North Carolina, she says, "I stayed with my sister and she got me in a drug treatment program. I started going to Narcotics Anonymous. I was attending meetings, but I found the people [in the meetings] were getting high, so it wasn't long before I was back on the drugs."

However, something good was waging war inside Janet against her drug-induced slave master. She enrolled in college and got a job. Things were beginning to look up, but not for long. Her longing . . . for love, for the father she never knew, for a husband . . . still drove her. She met a good-looking man who was very nice to her. She slept with him one time and got pregnant.

Then the drug-induced downward spiral began again, and she went out of control. "I actually went into labor while I was smoking crack," she remembers. "So I had the baby, and she was what you would call a preemie. She was underweight, so they wouldn't let me take her home . . . they didn't know that I had no place to take her anyway."

Her drug cravings made her lose all sense of responsibility, not only to the premature baby but to her one-year-old son as well. She went out searching to buy drugs and left her little boy with a local man. She was gone for a whole day, and when she returned, she couldn't find her son. The man whom she had left him with had become drunk and forgot he was watching a little boy. Now he was unable to find him.

Janet felt trouble closing in on her. What had she done? "He couldn't remember my name," she says. "He didn't know my baby's name. So his daughter called the police, and the Department of Social Services came and got my baby."

She continues. "I knew I was really in trouble now. I went home and just tried to block it out . . . I just got high. I stayed high for a total of nine days while they were looking for me."

Filled with guilt, deeply depressed, and tired of running, Janet turned herself in. Her cocaine master had more cruelty in store for this poor woman. She was convicted of child neglect and was sentenced to twelve to eighteen months in prison.

Imagine her anguish, her tears, and her soul searching. "I was sent to prison, and then my kids were separated and put in foster care. I didn't know who had my kids. It was very rough. I tried to explain to them that I really did love my kids, but I just didn't know how to get off of those drugs."

After serving just four months of her sentence, Janet was released from prison. Now she could go home and start over. However, just like before, Janet didn't have a home to go to. With tears in her eyes, she recalls those days. "I just lived from pillar to post, wherever. If I could spend a night here, I spent a night there. One time I took up residence in a crackhouse . . . and, in-between times of having nowhere to stay, it seemed like every six months I went to jail."

But God is a God of love and compassion. Was He answering the prayers of her dead mother or her beloved "Big Mama" who prayed when she was a little girl? Or did God see in Janet what Jesus saw in Mary Magdalene, from whom He cast out seven demons? Or was this lonely, drug-addicted prostitute like Rahab the harlot, whose name appears in the ancestry of the very Son of God?

While she was in jail, while working in a laundry room, a song on a radio became God's voice that transformed Janet's entire existence. Here's how she tells the story:

The very first song that came on the radio was a song by the Dallas-Fort Worth Mass Choir. It was called "Another Chance." When I heard that, some godly sorrow came over me. It convicted me.

I remember how I was standing there, folding the sheets and towels, and I just began to weep . . . and I just began to confess my sins to God, and I began to tell Him how sorry I was that I had lived so wickedly, and how I had been a prostitute, and how I almost destroyed this gift of life that He had given me. And I asked Him for one more chance!

I promised God in front of that radio. I said, "God, if You save me, I will serve You 'til I die." I knew that for God I would live and for God I would die.

I knew I was never going to use drugs and alcohol again. I knew I was never going to be a prostitute again. I knew I was never going to live that old wicked and sinful life again. The Word of God and the Spirit of the Lord are what has kept me these years.

And kept her He has. Janet is totally free from drug addiction and the rest of her destructive former life. She enrolled in Winston-Salem State University in North Carolina and graduated with honors in 2003. Two weeks later, she was offered a teaching position. She has been teaching for two and a half years in what she says is a fulfillment of a childhood dream.

Janet is a living, breathing miracle. The past has vanished, and for her all has become new. To top off her blessings, this former prostitute has been called by God to preach the gospel. She started out teaching the Bible in the local jail. She laughs when she says, "I knew that was God. One time I was crying, begging these people to let me out of jail, and now I am begging them to let me back in!"

Janet's wounds are healed, and she is trusting God to heal the wounds that she inflicted on her children. She admits, "I hurt my kids very deeply . . . and they probably have some questions. When the day comes when they are ready to ask me why, I'm prepared to sit down and try to answer their questions."

For now, God has healed the bitterness and lack of forgiveness in her oldest boy. "God," she says, "did a work in his life, so he and I have a very, very good relationship."

And so, to this family of four who were headed for degradation and destruction, God has sent His grace and His transforming power. As we think of Janet, our hearts echo the words of the prophet Isaiah, "Though your sins are like scarlet, they shall be as white as snow" (1:18)!

ANGELS AND DEMONS

The people of Gadara, known as Gadarenes, lived in an area southeast of the Sea of Galilee. Among these people was a wild man who roamed naked in the hills, screaming night and day and cutting himself with rocks. The people had tried to control him by capturing him and binding him with chains, but the man exhibited such supernatural strength that he snapped the chains and ran into the hills, where he continued to scream in torment night and day.

One day, Jesus Christ visited the area. When the wild man saw Him, he raced toward Jesus as if to do Him harm. Instead, as he drew near to Jesus, he dropped to the ground when Jesus commanded, "Come out of him." As the man knelt before Jesus, the spiritual beings that controlled him took over his voice and began pleading with Jesus. Jesus knew that He was dealing with demon spirits, so He stood boldly without fear and demanded, "What is your name?"

"Legion," came back the reply, "for we are many." (A Roman legion consisted of one thousand men.) Then these demons that without question recognized the power and authority of Jesus begged Him, "Please don't send us to the pit before the time."

"I give you permission to enter those swine," Jesus told them. With permission granted, the legion of demons left the man we know as the Gadarene demoniac and entered a herd of swine grazing nearby. When the demons entered them, the swine went crazy and rushed to their death in the waters of the lake (see Mark 5:1–13).

Demons were real in the days of Jesus, and demons are real today. The Bible tells us that Jesus gave His disciples power over demons and over "all the powers of hell" (Matthew 16:18 NLT).

WHAT ARE DEMONS AND WHAT DO THEY DO?

The pages of the Old and New Testaments contain numerous references to spiritual beings that were created by God before He created the human race. The most renowned of these beings was described by the prophet Ezekiel in a message not only directed toward the king of Tyre but clearly intended to describe someone infinitely more important:

You were the model of perfection, full of wisdom and perfect in beauty. You were in Eden, the Garden of God. . . . You were anointed as a guardian cherub, for so I ordained you. You were on the holy mount of God; you walked among the fiery stones. You were blameless in your ways from the day you were created till wickedness was found in you. Through your widespread trade you were filled with violence, and you sinned. So I drove you in disgrace from the mount of God, and I expelled you, O guardian cherub, from among the fiery stones. Your heart became proud on account of your beauty, and you corrupted your wisdom because of your splendor. So I threw you to the earth. (28:12–17 NIV)

Before He created our universe, Almighty God created a being named Lucifer, or "Light One," who possessed godlike wisdom, power, and beauty. The Bible says he was "the model of perfection" (v. 12 NIV). He was given the task, as an anointed cherub, of covering the very holiness of God. No greater splendor or authority had been given to any created being since creation.

What happened during that time is recorded by the prophet Isaiah in a message that is aimed at the king of Babylon, but it obviously transcends any earthly ruler:

> How have you fallen from heaven, O morning star, son of the dawn! You have been cast down to the earth, you who once laid low the nations! You said in your heart, "I will ascend to heaven; I will raise my throne above the stars of God. I will sit enthroned on the mount of assembly, on the utmost heights of the sacred mountain. I will ascend above the tops of the clouds; *I will make myself like the Most High.*" (14:12–14 NIV; emphasis added)

From the biblical record, we begin to understand that the beauty and splendor God gave to Lucifer was so magnificent that it overwhelmed (or, as Ezekiel says, "corrupted") his great wisdom. It led him to forget that everything he had was indeed a gift from the Creator.

It obviously led Lucifer to forget that the Creator is always more powerful than His creation, however splendid that creation may be. As Lucifer continued to contemplate his own abilities, his mind became warped with the thought that he was more capable of running the universe than was God. With that thought, pride (the root sin) and rebellion (pride's handmaid) entered the universe and forever corrupted it.

How pervasive today is human pride and arrogance, especially among the so-called intelligentsia of Western culture. Some months ago, I was involved in a discussion on cable channel CNBC on the role of the Ten Commandments in our society. My protagonist was Alan Dershowitz, who graduated from Yale Law School a couple of decades after me and is now a professor at Harvard Law School. I wondered if my ears had deceived me when I heard him say that the Ten Commandments were flawed and that he could do a better job of drafting a replacement set. Rather than answer him, I burst out laughing and said, "Only a Harvard law professor would claim publicly that he is smarter than God."

But this arrogance represents the pompous "intellectuals" who claim to know better than God how the world was created, how government is supposed to work and laws administered, how families are to be established and sexual relations conducted, and how we should manage our money, treat the poor, and educate the young.

Yes, pride and rebellion against God's authority underlie many of the actions of today's world leaders, philosophers, scientists, judges, and professors. And it was pride that corrupted Lucifer and caused him to be thrown out of heaven by a just and righteous God.

Before the creation of our material universe, God created, in addition to Lucifer, an entire class of beings called angels, who are agents or messengers of God. Angels are spiritual beings, splendid in appearance, that possess supernatural strength and wisdom. Sinful humanity does not have the capacity to see God except "through a glass, darkly" (1 Corinthians 13:12 KJV). Angels, on the other hand, "always see the face of [our] Father in heaven" (Matthew 18:10 NIV). Angels see God, and they know His voice and His will.

After Lucifer rebelled against God, he was no longer the perfect object of God's creation. Through the years, Jesus Christ and holy apostles and prophets have given him names that identify his character. He is called Satan, which means "the adversary" against God, against God's purposes, and against God's people; the devil, which comes from the Greek word *diabolos*, which means "lying accuser"; Beelzebub, the "prince of devils"; Abaddon or Apollyon, which means "the destroyer"; the great dragon or old serpent; the prince of the power of the air; and the prince or chief of this world.

In the twelfth chapter of the Book of Revelation, we read that the great dragon with his tail swept "a third of the stars [angels] out of the sky and flung them to the earth" (v. 4 NIV). In the same chapter we read, "There was war in heaven, Michael and his angels fought against the dragon, and the dragon and his angels fought back. But he was not strong enough, and they lost their place in heaven. The great dragon was hurled down—that ancient serpent called the devil, or Satan, who leads the whole world astray. He was hurled to the earth, and his angels with him" (vv. 7–9 NIV).

So the initial rebellion by Lucifer spread throughout the angels in heaven. From the twelfth chapter of Revelation, we can presume that a third of the angels joined the revolt. All we know for sure is that Jesus Christ spoke of a lake of fire "prepared for the devil and his angels" (Matthew 25:41), and Revelation tells us that the devil and his angels were hurled to earth (12:9).

WHAT ARE ANGELS AND WHAT DO THEY DO?

The angels that remained loyal to God are remarkably powerful spiritual beings. They appear from time to time to carry out God's will on earth. It is recorded that Jerusalem, in the days of King Hezekiah, was under life-threatening siege. In answer to the prayer of Hezekiah and the prophetic word of the prophet Isaiah, God sent one angel who single-handedly killed 185,000 of the Assyrian troops, which brought about the withdrawal of the remaining Assyrian forces and the assassination of the king of Assyria.

In New Testament times, severe persecution arose against the early Christian church. King Herod Agrippa began to persecute some of the believers, even to the extent of having James (the apostle John's brother) killed with the sword. During Passover, the king then arrested Peter with a plan to have him tried publicly after the Passover ended.

The church began praying earnestly for Peter. The Greek text indicates an agony of prayer. Acts 12:5 could be translated, "They prayed *stretch-outedly* for him."

Peter meanwhile was chained in prison, barefoot and dressed in a loincloth. His wrists were chained to soldiers on either side of him. Fourteen more soldiers were guarding his cell doors and the outer doors of the prison. Yet on the night before his trial began, Peter was sleeping soundly, despite his chains and the presence of his captors.

Suddenly, a light filled his cell and a deep sleep came upon all sixteen guards. An angel materialized out of the air and hit Peter on the side to wake him up. By supernatural power, Peter's chains fell off. Then the angel, in a very practical word of authority, commanded, "Get dressed. Put on your sandals. Put on your coat and follow me." Each locked door miraculously sprang open, and Peter and the angel walked through completely unnoticed by any of the prison guards until they had traversed the entire prison and come out onto the street. Then the angel left him. Up to this time, Peter had thought that he was dreaming. But when he found himself standing alone in the middle of the night on a city street, he realized that this was no dream.

He walked swiftly to the house where the disciples were praying for him. He knocked on the door. A servant girl opened the door, and when she saw Peter standing there, she was so frightened that she slammed the door in his face and ran to tell the others.

This was an answer to their prayer, but it seemed too good to be true. They exclaimed, "You're out of your mind. It must be his angel." The pounding on the door continued, and when they opened it, they realized that God had intervened and sent an angel to rescue Peter from the clutches of an evil tyrant (see Acts 12:6–17).

What does this tell us about angels? They are sent by God in answer to prayer. They are bright, luminous beings that can appear out of thin air and then vanish from sight. They are not constrained by what we know as solid matter. The enemies of God are helpless before them.

The Bible tells us that angels are "ministering spirits sent to serve those who will inherit salvation" (Hebrews 1:14 NIV). The number of angels is vast. In the Book of Revelation, John sees a vision of angels around God's throne and says that "the number of them was ten thousand times ten thousand [100 million], and thousands of thousands" (5:11).

The role assigned to angels in the last days is incredible. According to the Book of Revelation, angels control the trumpets, the bowls, and the vials of the unfolding judgment of the earth. They hold off judgment, and they unleash judgment. One angel is said to be powerful enough to hurl a flaming mountain into the ocean with such force that one-third of the ships are sunk (8:8–9). Four angels are released from the river Euphrates with power to kill one-third of mankind (9:14–15). Angels announce the doom of the Antichrist and the beginning of "the kingdom of our God, and the power of His Christ" (12:10). Angels are sent to thresh out of God's kingdom all those who are evildoers (Matthew 13:39–42).

John the Apostle, the author of the Book of Revelation, was so awestruck by the angel who had revealed the last things to him that he fell down to worship the angel, but the angel would not permit it. Here is the record of that exchange: "I, John . . . fell down to worship at the feet of the angel who had been showing them to me. But he said to me, 'Do not do it! I am a fellow servant with you and with your brothers the prophets and of all who keep the words of this book. *Worship God!*'" (Revelation 22:8–9 NIV; emphasis added). In this present age, we must welcome angels but never pray to them or worship them. Our worship must be to God Almighty and Him alone.

Angels ministered to Jesus after He was tempted by Satan. The Gospel of Mark tells us that Jesus "was in the desert forty days, being tempted by Satan. He was with the wild animals, and *angels attended him*" (1:13 NIV; emphasis added).

Angels were also present when Jesus wrestled in spiritual agony in the Garden of Gethsemane. When He was arrested just prior to His crucifixion, He boldly declared to His disciples, "Do you think I cannot call on my Father, and he will at once put at my disposal more than twelve legions of angels?" (Matthew 26:53 NIV). Twelve thousand angels would be enough power to kill every Roman soldier and take over the government of the world by force. But the way of God's kingdom is love and sacrifice, not force of arms.

The Bible also tells us that angels were with Jesus when He was tempted by Satan; angels were present when He wrestled in spiritual agony in the Garden of Gethsemane; and an angel came at Jesus's resurrection to roll the stone from the front of his tomb. Matthew describes the angel who appeared at the empty tomb: "His appearance was like lightning, and his clothes were white as snow. The guards were so afraid of him that they shook and became like dead men" (28:3–4 NIV). Throughout the Bible, the appearance of angels in their majesty and glory is so overwhelming as to bring on fear, weakness, fainting, and profound reverence.

Angels and Demons

With that in mind, what an amazing thought it is that, although human beings have been created "a little lower than the angels" (Psalm 8:5), when the end of the age comes and the angels are sent out to take from the kingdom of God all that offends, the Christian believers will, as part of the body of Christ, be crowned with glory and honor along with the Son of God, and given a place of authority for all eternity above the angels.

ANGELS PROVIDE MIRACULOUS PROTECTION

Many believe that each Christian believer is assigned a personal "guardian angel." I am not sure that this concept has explicit biblical authority. As we have seen, angels are "ministering spirits" sent to "those who will inherit salvation" (Hebrews 1:14). Does this mean that groups of angels look after groups of believers, like a zone defense in basketball; or is it one angel to one believer, like man-to-man coverage? We really don't know the answer, but we do know that much of the miraculous protection we experience in everyday life comes about because of the angels that are watching over us.

Stories have come out of the modern nation of Israel about battlefield miracles brought on by angels, like this remarkable account told me personally by Effie Eitam, a former Israeli Army brigadier general who has become an orthodox rabbi.

On Yom Kippur in 1973, the holiest day in the Jewish calendar, when almost all Jews were fasting and praying to seek atonement from God, the combined armies of Egypt, Syria, and Jordan launched an unprovoked attack on Israel. Israel's military reserves were hastily called from their prayers into their airplanes, battle tanks, half-tracks, and infantry units to repel hostile troops gathered at their borders. The flat plateau that becomes the Golan Heights extends from Damascus for about fifty miles before it drops off sharply to the rich agricultural Hula and Jordan valleys on the west, and to the Sea of Galilee and the city of Tiberius on the south.

The Syrians held all the high ground. Before their attack, they had amassed one thousand or more battle tanks on this high plateau, from which they could direct punishing artillery or mortar fire at the unprotected Jewish settlers living below.

The Israeli Defense Force had to rush to battle positions and then claw their way up the steep heights to confront the oncoming Syrians. Military historians have said that this was the fiercest tank battle since World War II in Europe.

Effie Eitam was a company commander who was ordered forward into this bitter, merciless struggle where men were dropping all around him. Then he received a nerve-chilling order: infiltrate the Syrian lines, make your way to the command post of the commanding general of the lead tank division, and kill or capture him.

This was a mission fraught with peril. The chances of success were almost nonexistent. But the peril to the nation was so great that boldness and daring were demanded. There was no time for restraint and caution. As Eitam led his company forward into the haze of battle smoke, he saw a bright being standing in the smoke. He thought it was a Syrian soldier guarding the division command post, so he raised his rifle to fire. Then, to his amazement, the figure turned into a dove that flew out of the smoke of battle straight at him.

The bird rested on the shoulder he needed to fire his weapon, so he brushed it away. It then fluttered over to his other shoulder, where it remained for the next ten days, occasionally fluttering to his outstretched hand, then back to his shoulder. The bird never left him during some of the most vicious tank, artillery, and hand-to-hand infantry fighting in the history of warfare.

Day after day, Eitam checked his unit for casualties. Day after day, not one man was killed or wounded. Day after day after day, while death and carnage were all around them, his unit suffered no casualties. Day after day, the dove stayed perched on his shoulder.

Finally, the Israeli forces drove deep across the Golan into Syrian territory. Eitam's unit had done its job, and it was reassigned to a rear echelon. As soon as the men began to move back to the safety of the rear, the dove flew away and was never seen again.

In biblical symbolism, the dove is the sign of the Holy Spirit. The dove with the olive branch in its beak was God's signal to Noah that the waters of the great flood had receded from the earth (Genesis 8:11). Throughout subsequent history, the dove with the olive branch has signified peace.

I believe that the dove that gave protection to the Israeli unit in the Yom Kippur War was actually an angel that chose not to present himself as a mighty warrior but as a symbol of peace, signifying that one day the hotly contested border of Israel will be part of a highway of peace.

As we have seen our attention must always be upon the Lord Himself. However, knowing the key roles angels have played throughout biblical history, it behooves us to acknowledge their existence and welcome their presence when they are sent to us from God, and to ask the Lord to send angels to come to our aid to overcome the forces of evil.

WHAT WILL HAPPEN TO DEMONS?

But what of the multitude of angels who followed Lucifer in his rebellion against God? As we have seen, the Bible tells us that the devil and his angels were cast to earth (Revelation 12:9). Jesus Christ, in what is called the parable of the sheep and the goats, says that the goats will be commanded, "Depart from me, you who are cursed, into the eternal fire prepared for the devil and his angels" (Matthew 25:41 NIV).

These fallen angels were cast out of heaven by the decree of Almighty God, and they and Lucifer were confined to earth. They came with great wrath, great hatred against God, and great hatred against human beings, who were made in the image of God.

These fallen angels—called devils, demons, or unclean spirits— know that they have a short time on earth, after which they will be condemned forever to a lake of fire or a bottomless pit. That is why the legion of unclean spirits that inhabited the Gadarene demoniac begged Jesus not to send them to the pit "before the time" (Matthew 8:29).

THE DECEPTIONS OF DEMONS

The Bible tells us that the devil is "a liar and the father of lies" (John 8:44 NIV). His agents on earth constantly spread lies. Devils are ceaselessly placing doubt in the minds of human beings about the nature of God and the goodness of God while they defame those who truly are serving Him. It appears that the demons' time on earth is spent devising means to seduce human beings into rebellion against God and devising systems to control human beings so these humans will commit acts which will bring the wrath of God against them.

Two of the most evil systems the world has ever known, Communism and Fascism, were brought into being by people who were controlled by demonic powers. Adolf Hitler and the Nazis were deeply involved in occult practices, and at least one secular commentator, William L. Shirer, in his book *The Rise and Fall of the Third Reich*, strongly suggests that

Hitler was demon possessed. Glimpses of certain writings of Karl Marx, the founder of Communism, also suggest that he was a satanist.

One feature of both Communism and Nazism that stands out is the enormous amount of effort made by both to spread lies. The Nazis had Joseph Goebbels, the very powerful and crafty minister of propaganda, and the Russian Communists had the three-billion-dollar-a-year Disinformation Bureau. Both of these agencies left no stone unturned to lie about their enemies, to cover up their own evil, and to manipulate public opinion in their own favor. It was called the technique of the Big Lie. And, for a time, it proved remarkably effective.

Jesus said of the devil, "He was a murderer from the beginning, not holding to the truth, for there is no truth in him. When he lies, he speaks his native language, for he is a liar and the father of lies" (John 8:44 NIV). These words express the essence of the devil and his fallen angels—they are murderers and liars.

There is no doubt in my mind that the seeming insanity of Muslim jihadists who sacrifice their own lives while slaughtering the innocent is actually the work of demons. I met in Jerusalem last year with an Arab Christian pastor who told me that people in his village near Galilee who made the *haj* or pilgrimage to Mecca often returned demon possessed. The whole concept of jihad—the "holy war" of killing and subjugating non-Muslims to Islam—and the fanaticism it spawns, has its origins, I believe, not in a holy God, but in the one who "was a murderer from the beginning" (John 8:44).

On earth, demons are disembodied spirits filled with unclean lusts. They desire to possess human bodies so they can experience through those bodies sensual and carnal experience. Demons are not constrained by the time span of one life, so they can bring to the minds of their victims what the Bible calls "familiar spirits," or experiences of family members in the present or in the past (Leviticus 19:31). Other demons can give "a spirit of divination," which is the power in limited fashion to tell the future (Acts 16:16).

DELIVERED FROM DEMONIC INFLUENCE

Demons can gain entrance into a human body if the intended victim uses drugs, tobacco, or alcohol. An addiction is greatly intensified by the presence of a demon.

I recall one notable instance that took place several decades ago. I had been invited by a group of Baptist men to lead a weekend retreat near Raleigh, North Carolina. On the last day, several of the men asked for prayer for various personal problems. One, an official in the Blue Cross organization in Virginia, asked for prayer to be able to break a twenty-five-year, pack-a-day tobacco habit. I remember the scene like it was yesterday. He sat on a chair in the center of the group, and I laid my hands on him. Speaking with a voice of authority, I said, "You spirit of nicotine, come out of him."

As I spoke that command, he coughed and a vile smell of stale tobacco came out of his mouth. It took less time for this man to be delivered than it takes to read about it. One command. One cough. One vile smell expelled. Then victory. This confirmed smoker was delivered from nicotine addiction instantly and has not smoked, to my knowledge, since that morning.

Was his addiction caused by the nicotine in the tobacco? In part. But the real force of his addiction was demonic. When the demon was cast out, the man was free.

Drug addiction, alcoholism, bizarre sex, masochism, suicidal thoughts, bipolar disorder, uncontrollable rages, urges to commit murder—all these have chemical causes, hormonal causes, and varied psychological causes; but in certain instances, they are either heightened by demon influence or originated by demons.

At CBN, our expanded building featured, to the right side of the lobby, a prayer room with a wooden cross suspended from the apex of a vaulted ceiling over a large rock on which we had placed a pulpit-sized Bible. Sectional wooden benches were placed in concentric circles around the cross, the rock, and the Bible. Our staff met there for prayer, but if someone came to the lobby in need of prayer, he or she could be easily escorted by a minister into the prayer room.

A fifteen-year-old girl came one day, seeking help to get rid of voices telling her to kill her mother. The receptionist called me to help this teenager, and I asked for the assistance of a dedicated member of our ministerial staff.

We were impressed by the appearance of a perfectly normal, attractive, dark-haired girl. "Tell me your problem," I said.

She replied calmly, "When I am at home, there are voices in my head telling me to kill my mother."

"How often do you hear these voices?" I asked.

"All the time when I am at home," she replied.

"Has your mother ever been cruel to you in any way?" I probed further.

"No," she replied. "I love my mother. She has always been very good to me."

"She doesn't yell at you or hit you?"

"She gets mad at me sometimes, but not often."

"When did these feelings begin?" I continued.

"Something came over me about six months ago," she remembered.

"Then I started hearing the voices trying to force me to kill my mother. I don't know what's happening, but I am scared I might do something bad. Please help me."

My associate and I asked a few more questions until we were convinced that we were dealing with a spirit of murder that had taken over this child. How it got there we were unable to find out.

She wanted prayer, and we were more than willing to pray for her to be set free. We began to pray and very little happened. Finally, the two of us agreed with great intensity and ordered this spirit of murder to come out of this child in the name of Jesus. We were prepared to spend the rest of the day and the coming night until that evil spirit obeyed.

Suddenly, we won the battle. The girl began to choke and retch. As we alternated between praising God and commanding the demon, it came out of her and she was free. She smiled happily at us, and we smiled back as we praised the Lord for this great victory. We made sure that she had given her heart to Jesus Christ, and then we left her.

As a postscript, the following summer I happened to encounter this youngster in Virginia Beach. She seemed very happy. "How is it between you and your mother?" I asked.

"Everything is fine," she replied.

"No more thoughts of killing her?" I asked.

"Oh, no, they are all gone," was the answer. "I love my mother."

THE DANGER OF DELIVERANCE MINISTRIES

I am not particularly impressed by so-called deliverance ministries that seem to major in casting out real or imagined demons. I believe that it is a grave mistake to attribute every illness, misfortune, and psychological malady to demon power. Untrained people, including Christian ministers, can do great harm to diseased or mentally ill people when they add to their problems by telling them they are demon possessed, as this next story clearly illustrates.

My wife and I were visiting Israel with a very large group from the United States. We were staying at the Intercontinental Hotel on the Mount of Olives in Jerusalem. Before leaving for the large evangelistic meeting one night, we stopped in the hotel coffee shop for a quick snack. As we were eating, three or four middle-aged women in the group came to our table with a pitiful story. "Brother Robertson," they began, "a lady in our group is in terrible shape. She is in her room, crying out in torment. Why don't you get some of the men and go cast the demons out of her?"

I was late for the meeting, so I remained noncommittal and left as soon as I could. But these ladies would not be denied. The next evening, we were sitting at the same table when they returned. "Oh, brother," they cried out, "she is desperate. She is crying out to die. She was making so much noise that we moved her to another hotel. Please go see her."

I couldn't refuse a request like this, so I got the woman's name and her hotel. Then Dede and I got a cab and traveled to a smaller hotel closer to downtown. I got the woman's room number from the front desk, and my wife and I went up to her door and rang the bell. A tall, thin woman of some forty-five years of age with coal black hair and the look of a hunted animal in her eyes opened the door.

I identified myself and asked if we could come in. She and Dede sat on the only two chairs, and I sat on the edge of the bed. I skipped the small talk and immediately explored the problem that was facing her.

She said, "I have asthma that is so severe that I can't breathe. Sometimes it feels that I am dying."

"Have you seen a doctor?" I asked. She nodded. "What did he tell you?"

Her face was somber when she said, "My doctor says that my asthma is caused by praying with nuns."

I almost fell off the bed. "Do you mean to tell me that a licensed doctor actually told you that your asthma was caused by praying with nuns?"

"That is exactly what he told me," she replied.

I, of course, knew that this diagnosis was as phony as the assumptions of the ladies at the hotel that this tormented woman's asthma was a sign of demon possession. I was at a loss how to proceed, so I closed my eyes and said a silent prayer: *Lord, what is wrong with this woman?* The answer came quickly: "Ask her about her sex life."

Regardless of such an instruction, I had no intention of asking a total stranger about her sex life. So I hedged, "Tell me about your marriage."

"I have a wonderful marriage," she replied confidently. "My husband and I have been married for some time, and my marriage is good."

Another dead end, and another silent prayer. *Lord, what is the matter with her?*

Again the same answer: "Ask her about her sex life."

So I fumbled, fidgeted, and with profound apology finally asked this total stranger, "How is your sex life?"

She replied demurely, "I don't have any sex life."

"Why not?" I asked. "I thought you said you have a wonderful marriage."

"For the past two years, my husband has been impotent," she responded.

Now it doesn't take a psychological genius to know that praying with nuns doesn't cause asthma, but a marriage with no sex and an impotent husband can. Of course, the Lord in His wisdom knew the problem all along, and in about seven minutes He had shown me what it was.

"And you think that your husband's impotence is your fault, don't you?"

"Yes, I do," she said tearfully. "I blame myself."

"Well, it's not your fault," I said reassuringly. "He may be working too hard with lots of stress. He may have a physical problem. But whatever caused the problem, it wasn't you!"

"Are you sure?" she asked quietly.

"Absolutely sure," I replied. "Now, let's pray for God to heal your asthma." And pray we did. In a few moments, God's power touched this woman. Her face lit up with joy. All traces of the asthma were gone. We left her and went on to the evening meeting.

Just imagine what a downward spiral I could have put this woman in if I had barged into her room, told her she was full of demons, placed my hand on her forehead, and screamed, "Devil, in the name of Jesus, come out of this woman!" Fortunately, God sent me and my wife, instead of people who may have been determined to cast out demons.

POWER TO OVERCOME THE ENEMY

As we turn our attention back to the life of Jesus in the Bible, we see that the first miracle of Jesus recorded in the Gospel of Mark occurred at the synagogue in Capernaum on the shore of the Sea of Galilee. As Jesus was teaching on the Sabbath, He was confronted by a demon-possessed man:

A man in their synagogue who was possessed by an evil spirit cried out, "What do you want with us, Jesus of Nazareth? Have you come to destroy us? I know who you are—the Holy One of God."

"Be quiet!" said Jesus sternly. "Come out of him." The evil spirit shook the man violently and came out of him with a shriek.

The people were all so amazed that they asked each other,

"What is this? A new teaching—and with authority! He even gives orders to evil spirits and they obey him." (Mark 1:23–27 NIV)

When demons, then and now, are in the presence of the power of God, they invariably must manifest themselves. Last spring, I was in New Delhi, India, speaking to a crowd in an outdoor field of between fifty and seventy-five thousand people, the majority of whom were either Muslim or Hindu. As I spoke about Jesus, disturbances would break out in the crowd. Some would be convulsed, some would cry out, and others involuntarily performed strange, compulsive acts. I knew that I was witnessing the manifestation of demons trying to flee the name of Jesus, so I continued preaching until an invitation to receive Jesus Christ as Lord brought tens of thousands to faith.

Christians must understand the power that exists in the name of Jesus. His mandate of authority has been given to us: "As you go, preach this message: 'The kingdom of heaven is near.' Heal the sick, raise the dead, cleanse those who have leprosy, *drive out demons*" (Matthew 10:7–8 NIV; emphasis added); "I have given you authority to trample on snakes and scorpions and *to overcome all the power of the enemy*; nothing will harm you. However, do not rejoice that *the spirits submit to you*, but rejoice that your names are written in heaven" (Luke 10:19–20 NIV; emphasis added).

I have learned over the years that the fallen angels have ranks of power and authority. The prophet Daniel was told by an angel that he, the angel, had been hindered on his way to answer Daniel's prayer by "the prince of Persia" (Daniel 10:20). Certain powerful demons have rule over nations; others rule cities. In certain Eastern countries, the demons have names and are worshiped as gods. In India, two of the most powerful are Shiva, the male god of destruction and renewal, and

Kali, the female goddess of destruction and renewal. In Thailand, the ruling deity is known as the Lord of Siam and is only approached once a year by the king.

How can victory be gained in these areas? Jesus spoke of binding the strong man. "How can anyone enter a strong man's house and carry off his possessions unless he first ties up the strong man? Then he can rob his house" (Matthew 12:29 NIV). Before CBN begins broadcasting in certain areas, we speak these words: "Satan, I bind you and the forces of evil in the name of Jesus."

Sometimes people wonder why particular tragedies or human failings seem to be prevalent in certain areas of the United States. The answer is often found in the influence of the demonic prince who controls parts of the spiritual life in the city or the region.

Some years ago, when our television network was expanding, I heard of a television station broadcasting in the Seattle-Tacoma area of Washington that was available for sale at a very reasonable price. I traveled to Seattle and concluded a very successful negotiation to buy the station from its owner. We finished our business too late to catch a plane back east, so I secured a room for the night at a motel that adjoined the former Sea-Tac Airport.

I slept comfortably, but in the early morning hours as I lay in that sort of twilight between sleep and waking, something strange began to happen to my thoughts. Waves of betrayal, hopelessness, and despair began to fill my half-awake mind. I struggled to gain waking consciousness, and as soon as I did, without hesitation I spoke out into the darkness, "You spirit of suicide, in Jesus's name, I command you to leave." And leave me it did. I was once again my usual optimistic self, ready for a new day.

Years later, I can still remember that terrible feeling brought on by the being that tried to push my mind into hopelessness and despair. I checked out of the motel, traveled to the nearby airport, and was soon winging my way back to the East Coast. Later I learned that Seattle, in the days before Microsoft, had gained the title of "suicide capital of America." Had I realized the character of the controlling demon prince, I could have saved myself a great deal of trouble by binding the reigning strong man before I arrived in the city.

WHEN DEMONIC POWERS GAIN AN ENTRANCE

God normally protects innocent human beings from demonic attacks and invasions. But when people violate what they know to be right, demonic powers can gain an entrance, as this next story illustrates.

In the early 1960s, a kind and generous man offered my family and me the free use of a lovely old farmhouse in the country. As our children reached high school age, they joined a Christian church group and then asked if they could turn the garage on the property into a Christian "coffeehouse."

We readily agreed and soon were delighted that upwards of one hundred teenagers were spending Friday and Saturday nights praising the Lord in our garage-turned-"coffeehouse."

One Friday night, I worked late and did not come home until about nine o'clock. I was fixing myself a bite to eat when, at nine fifteen, there was a knock at the kitchen door. Three teenagers asked if I could come outside to help a young girl who was in trouble. I went with them down the drive to the white fence enclosing a pasture, then down the road along the fence toward the old red barn on the property.

In the light from a single light pole, I could make out the form of a diminutive seventeen-year-old girl sitting on the ground near the fence. A couple of students from the coffeehouse crowd were with her.

I bent down and asked her what was the matter.

She said, "I've been down there, but I can't stand the praying."

"Why not?" I asked.

"When they pray, something starts jumping in my stomach, and a voice tells me to get out!"

I clarified, "You say when they pray, something starts jumping inside you?"

"Yes," she answered. "I just can't stand it."

I said, "Would you mind if I prayed for you now?"

"Oh, no," she protested. "No prayer. I can't stand it!"

I knew that this girl's reaction to the very sincere faith of her fellow students was not normal. People can certainly be turned off by any form of worship, but violent physical manifestations and voices indicate the presence of the power of evil. Somehow, this diminutive seventeen-year-old had managed to become demon possessed, and I wanted to help her schoolmates get her free.

I began to pray, and she became violent. Two of the teenagers held her arms while I commanded the demon to come out of her. She exhibited almost superhuman strength and screamed at the top of her lungs, "Let me go!"

I addressed the demon. "Satan, I won't let you go. I command you in the name of Jesus Christ to come out of her."

Then it happened. The girl's voice became deeper, and the strange voice coming out of her said, "You can't have her. She's mine. We've won. We've won."

I said, "You're a liar, Satan. Jesus Christ has won. Come out!"

Then I remembered the words of Jesus, who said, "This kind can come out only by prayer" (Mark 9:29 NIV). So I prayed a quick, silent prayer: *Father, You've got to help me. Please get this thing out of her.*

Suddenly, the girl relaxed and opened her eyes. The evil spirit had left her, but she had no memory of what had been taking place and no recollection of the words that had come out of her mouth.

"How do you feel?" I asked.

"I feel fine," she answered.

"Would you like to join the other kids at the prayer meeting?" I asked.

She smiled very happily and answered, "I'd like to very much!" So off she went to enjoy the rest of the night, and I went back to the house to finish dinner.

I later learned that, while visiting out of state, this teenager had gone to an X-rated movie. It was there that the demonic being felt it gained permission to overtake her and possess her. It was intent on destroying this precious child created in the image of God, but God had different plans that He made clear during that encounter near the white board fence on the side of a country pasture on a balmy summer's night.

This encounter was not the Hollywood version of any exorcism. I commanded in the name of Jesus. The demon resisted. I prayed a brief prayer for help. Then the demon left. The victim began to praise Jesus. Case closed. None of the priestly suicides and weirdness of the movies. Just another miracle flowing from the mandate given by Jesus to all believers: "Heal the sick . . . raise the dead, cast out demons" (Matthew 10:8).

If you are filled with His Spirit, you can be encouraged by Jesus's words: "All things *are* possible to him who believes" (Mark 9:23). Power over fallen angels is miraculous, but that miraculous power can be yours in Jesus's name.

THE DEAD ARE RAISED

Easter is a day of celebration for Christians all over the world. They greet one another that day by calling out, "He is risen!" And the joyful answer comes back, "He is risen indeed!"

When Jesus died on a Roman cross, He became the atoning sacrifice for the sins of each one of us. The beating He experienced was for the healing of our sicknesses and diseases. The Bible tells us, "By His stripes we are healed" (Isaiah 53:5).

Jesus's excruciating death would have been in vain if He had not come back from the dead. Without the resurrection, Jesus would have taken His place among the tragic martyrs of history who suffered and died at the hands of cruel tyrants.

But the resurrection changed all of that. Jesus is not a tragic figure, beaten and crucified, to be honored only for His sacrifice. Instead, Jesus has been raised triumphant. He is alive forevermore. As He promised, He is with those who believe in Him "even to the end of the age" (Matthew 28:20). Eternal salvation comes to an individual who personally receives the death of Jesus Christ as an atoning sacrifice for sin and then takes the second step of making the risen Christ the Lord of his or her life.

HOW DO PEOPLE COME BACK FROM THE DEAD?

There are two ways that people come back from the dead. In the case of Jesus Christ, it was a resurrection. He came back in a new body . . . a spiritual body able to materialize in the middle of a closed room and then disappear from sight; to eat a meal and have real flesh-and-blood wounds examined by skeptical disciples yet be transported into heaven in an instant; a new body that was immortal, one that would never grow old or die again.

Resurrection

For Christian believers, our resurrection will not occur until Jesus Christ returns to earth, at which time those who are dead will be clothed with spiritual bodies like that of Jesus, and those who are alive will be instantly changed.

The words of the apostle Paul on the subject of our future resurrection are worth repeating:

> I want to remind you of the gospel I preached to you . . . that Christ died for our sins according to the Scriptures, that he was buried, that he was raised on the third day according to the Scriptures. . . .
>
> But if it is preached that Christ has been raised from the dead, how can some of you say that there is no resurrection of the dead? If there is no resurrection of the dead, then not even Christ has been raised. And if Christ has not been raised, our preaching is useless and so is your faith. . . . And if Christ has not been raised, your faith is futile; you are still in your sins. Then those also who have

fallen asleep in Christ are lost. If only for this life we have hope in Christ, we are to be pitied more than all men. (1 Corinthians 15:1, 3–4, 12–14, 17–19 NIV)

So resurrection by the power of God is the future for every Christian believer. This transformation is the greatest miracle of all. If asked, almost every Christian will emphatically state that he or she will be part of the resurrection. I marvel at those who believe without any doubt that at the last days every one of the trillion cells in their bodies will be miraculously transformed into an ever-youthful spiritual body capable of transcending space and time, yet they cannot believe that God will in today's world heal a simple cancer, brain tumor, or arthritis of the hands.

The apostle Paul amplified in some detail what he thinks will happen:

Someone may ask, "How are the dead raised? With what kind of body will they come?" How foolish! What you sow does not come to life unless it dies. When you sow, you do not plant the body that will be, but just a seed, perhaps of wheat or of something else. But God gives it a body as he has determined, and to each kind of seed he gives its own body. . . . There are also heavenly bodies and there are earthly bodies; but the splendor of the heavenly bodies is one kind, and the splendor of the earthly bodies is another. . . .

So will it be with the resurrection of the dead. The body that is sown is perishable, it is raised imperishable; it is sown in dishonor, it is raised in glory; it is sown in weakness, it is raised in power; it is sown a natural body, it is raised a spiritual body. . . .

I declare to you, brothers, that flesh and blood cannot inherit the kingdom of God, nor does the perishable inherit the imperishable.

Listen, I tell you a mystery: We will not all sleep, but we will all be changed—in a flash, in the twinkling of an eye, at the last trumpet. For the trumpet will sound, the dead will be raised imperishable, and we will be changed. (1 Corinthians 15:35–38, 40, 42–44, 50–52 NIV)

Resurrection! The perishable changed into imperishable. Bodies like those of angels. We will then be like Jesus, for "we shall see Him as He is" (1 John 3:2). This is our hope! Resurrection is the greatest miracle for each of us, but that miracle is for the end of days.

Resuscitation

Jesus gave His disciples the authority to raise the dead *now*—not to bring them to the resurrection of the dead at the end of days, but to resuscitate them, to bring them back again to their human condition after they have died.

In ancient days, there was a village in the Galilee area about two miles south of Mount Tabor and a short distance southwest of the Sea of Galilee. According to Luke's Gospel:

Jesus went to a town called Nain, and his disciples and a large crowd went along with him. As he approached the town gate, a dead person was being carried out—the only son of his mother, and she was a widow. . . . When the Lord saw her, his heart went out to her and he said, "Don't cry."

Then he went up and touched the coffin, and those carrying it stood still. He said, "Young man, I say to you, get up!" The dead man sat up and began to talk, and Jesus gave him back to his mother.

The Dead Are Raised

They were all filled with awe and praised God. "A great prophet has appeared among us," they said. (7:11–16 NIV)

What happened to this boy in Nain? When a person's body dies, his immortal spirit departs and begins a journey. Jewish tradition in Jesus's time said that the spirit remained near the body for three days before it departed to its final rest. Jesus told a thief dying on the cross next to Him, "Today you will be with Me in Paradise" (Luke 23:43). Wherever the boy's spirit was—Abraham's bosom, Paradise, or Hades—Jesus called it back into his body: "Young man, I say to you, get up!"

In order for the body to "get up," his spirit had to return, and all of the young man's bodily functions—his heart, his brain, his circulation, his other vital organs—all had to start up again without any ill effects from the shutdown of his entire body and without the ill effects of whatever had killed him in the first place.

At Jesus's command, all of this took place in an instant. Death could not resist the command of the Son of God, because the Bible tells us that "in Him was life, and the life was the light of men" (John 1:4). Jesus Christ is the source of life, and He is able to impart life in the same way that the Father imparted life on the day of creation.

But neither Lazarus nor the son of the widow of Nain was resurrected to a new life. Each was *resuscitated* from death to the same life as before, and each would experience ultimate physical death sometime in the future. The authority Jesus gives to His disciples is not to bring about resurrections, for the resurrection of the body is reserved exclusively for the time set by the Father. We have received a mandate of authority to resuscitate back to physical life those who have died.

SHOULD WE PRAY TO STOP DEATH?

What constitutes death or near death and whether we should intervene is highlighted in this account from Bogotá, Columbia.

In 1968, I flew from Norfolk, Virginia, to Bogotá, Columbia, and purchased for our missionary purposes an AM radio station known as Emissora Nuevo Continente. We installed a young Christian bank manager named Dario Quiroga as the station manager and began broadcasting our *700 Club* program on the station with a new name, *Momentos de Gozo y Alabanza* ("Moments of Joy and Praise"). Nuevo Continente broadcast a mix of Latin favorites that achieved good audience ratings. Better still, *Momentos* was extremely popular, with wonderful spiritual results.

The affairs of the station marched along with less-than-wonderful financial results for a couple of years. One day, I received word that Dario Quiroga, our manager, was at death's door. He had developed an infection in his nose that had spread to his brain. Now he was lying in a coma with brain fever, hanging between life and death.

I arranged to fly to South America. I changed planes in Panama, where I was joined by Sixto Lopez, an American missionary who was the ministry leader at Nuevo Continente. We journeyed together to Bogotá, and we finally got into our hotel rooms in the early morning. We met for breakfast and began discussing the spiritual implications of praying for Dario, of keeping him from death. Was this prayer in God's will?

"Do you suppose the Lord wants to take him?" I asked Sixto.

We agreed that it would seem that God would want to heal this young father of five. Yet we weren't sure what God's will was. Perhaps He had a higher and better course for Dario. Sixto then told me a story of an acquaintance who was crying out to God to restore to life his dying friend. Sixto said, "In the middle of the prayer, God stopped him and said, 'Let him die.' So he stopped praying, and while he was still on his knees, he sensed the spirit of his friend pass behind him and leave the house. When he went into the bedroom, there lay the lifeless body. The spirit of his friend had departed according to God's direction."

I said, "We certainly don't want to fight God. So if God wants to take Dario, let's not hurry. Let's have another cup of tea and let him get good and dead. But if he's alive when we get to the hospital, we will pray for his healing."

So Sixto and I talked, drank tea, and waited, according to our imperfect wisdom, so that God had time to act. Then we decided we had waited long enough and should go to the hospital. When we entered Dario's room, the nurse motioned us aside and whispered, "He's hopeless. If he wakes up, he will be a vegetable." We were now on a mission, and this tidbit of negativity did not deter us at all.

Dario was lying on the hospital bed faceup, completely unconscious and motionless, except for his labored breathing. Sixto stood on one side of the bed, and I stood on the other. We laid our hands on Dario's chest and forbade the death angel to take him. I prayed in English and commanded a healing. Sixto prayed in Spanish and cried out to God to heal our unconscious friend. At the end of his prayer, Sixto said, "Amen."

And wonder of wonders, Dario's spirit surfaced, threw off the shackles of illness and death, and said, "Amen." He opened his eyes and greeted us. God had healed him in answer to our prayers. We all praised God for His miracle. In answer to the nurse's dire warnings, I remarked with a smile, "Dario is the only bilingual vegetable I've ever met."

RETURN FROM DEATH'S DOOR

It was Sunday morning, December 30, 2001. In an attractive home in Vicksburg, Mississippi, Tommy Davis, the husband of teacher's assistant

Connie Davis, was in the kitchen of their home making coffee before taking Connie and their son to church. He heard a sickening thud in the bedroom and rushed upstairs to find out what had happened. He found his young wife, age forty-one, lying unconscious. He grabbed a telephone and made a frantic call for help.

Within minutes, the paramedics arrived and rushed Connie to the emergency room at the River Regional Medical Center. In truth, Connie was dead when she hit the floor at home. The hospital doctors discovered that Connie had suffered a pulmonary embolism—a blood clot that hit her lung. The trauma from that clot left Connie without blood pressure or pulse. In the words of an intensive care nurse, "Her eyes were open and looking at me, but they weren't looking. Quite frankly, I was looking at a dead person."

When Connie arrived at the hospital, it turned out that some of the most skilled doctors in Vicksburg were on duty that day. The emergency room staff worked on Connie for an unusually long time—one and a half hours. Although she couldn't respond, Connie heard the doctors announcing their grim prognosis. None of them gave her any hope of survival. One even said that they would learn more about her condition "after the autopsy."

Word of Connie's collapse had reached her Triumph Church, because some of the church elders had been conducting their regular hospital ministry visit when Connie was brought in. They rushed back to the church, where the morning service was in progress, and told the congregation that Connie's life was literally hanging in the balance. Pastor Mike Fields stopped the service, and the entire congregation of some four hundred people began praying for Connie. Some of the church's special intercessors left the service and drove to the hospital.

At the hospital, Dr. Bob Ford related his efforts to revive Connie. "We had a heart doctor, a lung doctor, and different doctors coming in and different people doing the code [a term used in the hospital to describe an attempt to resuscitate a person with no vital signs]. Basically, we never were able to regain a blood pressure, pulse, or any objective evidence that she was breathing or alive."

That's when intensive care nurse Joyce Langston got the call to bring one of the strongest blood pressure medicines to the emergency room—a medicine of last resort. In her words, "They had not been able to get any pulse, had not gotten any blood pressure. And she wasn't responding to any of the medicines."

Dr. Ford said that they had gone to extreme measures, but to no avail. The last act of the medical staff was to call the time of death. In Dr. Ford's words, "She was clinically dead. They had called the code [called the time of death] and pronounced her dead."

But what the hospital staff did not realize was that Connie's friends, her family, and her church had begun to storm heaven on her behalf. Not only was the church in the sanctuary interceding for Connie, praying against death and praying for life, the intercessors in the hospital, along with Connie's husband, had asked permission to enter the emergency room and pray.

They gathered around, laid hands on Connie's lifeless body, and began to barrage heaven with their prayers. One member, Thelma Russell, vividly remembers what happened. "When I laid hands on her she was cold. I said, 'Lord, with long life You promised to satisfy her. Lord, You said You would do her good and not evil, that You would give her an expected end, that Your will for her is to live and not die." To those members of Connie's church in the emergency room, those words became a chorus: "Live and not die."

Suddenly, as if by a miracle, Connie began gripping her husband's hand. Thelma Russell's hand began to feel what she describes as a "sort of shivering" on Connie's lifeless body as life was coming back into her.

Connie Davis was breathing. Her blood pressure was rising. Doctors and nurses were stunned—including one nurse who had helped with CPR. Nurse Joyce Langston recalled her reaction. "I have been doing this for twenty-eight years, and I have never seen anything like it. After these people prayed, she got a pulse."

As Dr. Ford tells it, "Well, all I know is the family went in, and when they came out, the nurses went back in there and she was spontaneously starting to breathe again, and we began feeling blood pressure and a pulse again."

But it would take more than blood pressure and a pulse. Connie still faced an uphill battle. Besides all of her major organs shutting down, Connie showed no signs of brain activity.

Dr. Ford continued the account. "We knew she was brain dead when she started back. She had no spontaneous activity. She was on a ventilator. She had aspiration pneumonia, which means she aspirated her stomach contents during CPR. We broke her ribs. Her kidneys went into failure from a lack of oxygen. She just had every complication that you can have from a cardiac arrest."

But God is not controlled by incontrovertible medical evidence. Connie's friends and church members had no intention of stopping their prayers. They bombarded heaven and cried out for a miracle.

About four o'clock the next afternoon, two nurses attending Connie began to notice unusual things. The respiratory therapist was beside the bed and called out to the ER nurse, "Joyce, I think she's sticking her tongue out at me!"

Joyce shot back, "Donna, she's brain dead; she's not sticking her tongue out at you!"

The Dead Are Raised

About that time, Connie started shaking her head. Joyce went around the bed and asked in total disbelief, "Are you awake?" Connie answered by a nod of her head.

Joyce was dumbfounded. "I thought, you know, this just can't be. This is a mistake. When she came over, her body temperature was 89.9 degrees. She was already headed out. Her body was starting to cool off. So I'm just thinking this just can't be. This kind of stuff doesn't happen. She could move her legs and everything. No neurological defects."

But even more amazing things began to unfold. At three o'clock the next morning—just fifteen hours after she was to be officially pronounced dead, Connie wrote a note to her husband, reminding him of a doctor's appointment he had the next day.

As Connie's miracle progressed, Joyce knew exactly where to turn as various medical emergencies arose. With a sense of joy and awe, she recalls those moments. "At every turn, I would go out there and there was this sea of people from Connie's church in the waiting room, and I would find Mike and Tommy. I said, 'You all need to be praying. She's bleeding, and I can't get the bleeding stopped.' And they would pray.

At the end of thirty days, Connie Davis left the hospital—restored body and mind to perfect health! A living, breathing miracle. "She's beautiful. She's vibrant. She's full of life and so full of the joy of the Lord. And it is incredible to contemplate that she is the dead woman I saw in the emergency room," Joyce Langston exclaimed.

As Dr. Bob Ford muses over Connie's case, he believes what happened was truly a miracle. "There's no way physiologically," he says, "to explain how someone can go two hours in a code and not get blood supply to the brain like she did or blood to the kidneys and come out of it neurologically fine. I've never seen it before. The fact that she came out without any damage at all is truly a miracle."

Connie Davis's husband, Tommy, expresses the thoughts of all those who participated in Connie's miracle. "I heard often that God did a lot of stuff in the Bible back in the days of old. But I know now that He is a miracle worker, and He does raise people from the dead because He raised my wife from the dead! I was there, and I know!"

While she was physically dead, her spirit was very much present. Connie was aware of what was going on around her and what people were saying. She could see her body convulsing and foam coming from her mouth. She remembers what the doctors were saying and remembers watching them treat her. She doesn't really know whether this was an out-of-body experience. She does know that she realized, from what she heard, that she was going to die, so she made sure that she was right with the Lord. She prayed the sinner's prayer. She prayed the Twenty-third Psalm. She remembers saying, "Father, if You really don't need me, I really would like to raise my son."

Then, when the intercessors arrived for what the doctors thought was a last farewell, Connie heard their prayers as they asked for a miracle. Just then, Connie felt a "blinding light" hit her, and her body jumped. She squeezed her husband's hand, and her pulse and blood pressure returned. That blinding light was clearly the power of God pouring life into a lifeless body in answer to believing prayer.

PERSEVERE IN PRAYER

We can learn a great lesson from Connie's experience. When Jesus Christ was on earth, He raised the dead with a faith command: "Lazarus, come forth!" "Young man, I say to you, get up!" "Little girl, arise!" Nothing more, just a simple command backed up by faith in the awesome power of God Almighty. For us, whose faith is so imperfect, who see the spiritual world so dimly, more is often needed.

Jesus's disciples felt this need clearly, so they came to Him with a request: "Lord, teach us to pray" (Luke 11:1). In response, Jesus gave them a model prayer that has become known as the Lord's Prayer (vv. 2–4). He then went beyond the model prayer to make them understand the importance of importunity or persistence when they prayed.

He told them a story about a man and his family who had retired for the night in their one-bedroom house (vv. 5–8). The lights were out, the door was locked, and the family was sound asleep. Suddenly, they were awakened by a loud banging on their front door. Groggily, the homeowner looked out his small upstairs window. There was his neighbor knocking away. "Leave me alone," he called out. "My family and I are in bed." Then he slammed the window.

But the loud knocking continued. "Are you deaf?" the homeowner shouted. "I told you I am not getting up. Go away!"

But still more knocking. Now the noise was waking up the adjoining neighbors, so the wide-awake homeowner called out, "Be quiet. What do you want?"

"A friend has come from a journey, and I have nothing to give him to eat. Please lend me three loaves of bread."

Grumbling and very annoyed, the homeowner stumbles downstairs in the dark, grabs three flat rounds of bread from the cupboard, shoves them into the hands of his neighbor, slams the door in his face, and trudges back to bed.

Jesus said that the neighbor did not get the bread because of friendship or the nature of his appeal. He got the bread because his neighbor refused to quit asking. His prayer was answered because of what the King James Bible calls "importunity"—insistent solicitation and entreaty (v. 8).

Consequently, Jesus told us to ask, to seek, and to knock (v. 9). In the Greek language, the present tense of a verb implies continuous action. So the literal meaning of Jesus's instruction is to "keep on asking," and you will receive. "Keep on seeking," and you will find that for which you are looking. "Keep on knocking," and the door will be opened to you.

In short, in spiritual matters, the prize is awarded for perseverance. The careless, unstable, indifferent person will never win, either in the material world or in the spiritual.

Connie Davis's husband and her church were not about to pray a "little prayer" and quit. They declared life; they rebuked death; they pled the promises of the Bible; they kept on asking, kept on seeking, and kept on knocking until Connie was not just partially resuscitated but brought back to life and completely and totally healed.

Jesus told Mary and Martha, as they wept over the death of their brother Lazarus, "I am the resurrection and the life. He who believes in me will live, even though he dies; and whoever lives and believes in me will never die" (John 11:25–26 NIV).

BREAD FOR EACH DAY

Throughout history, the human race has been plagued by a shortage of food, caused by droughts, insect infestation, and natural and man-made disasters. These famines have resulted in the deaths of hundreds of thousands and even the migration of entire populations or the collapse of civilizations. From one point of view, the entire history of humanity could be written as a chronicle of economic survival—essentially having enough food to sustain life.

Even in the modern world, a slang term for currency is "bread." Bread is still the catch phrase for the food we need to keep us alive, and the common parlance describing employment is "earning a living"—in essence, earning enough money to purchase the food, clothing, and shelter necessary to sustain life. People need food to stave off starvation, so having enough money to store up food supplies is an obvious solution to a temporary shortage of food or an outright famine.

As civilization progressed, the acquisition of more and more money became an end in itself—not to avoid famine and death, but as a mark of achievement, a source of pride. Money became a type of scoreboard of comparison with others, coldly computed on bank statements, brokerage reports, and asset ledgers. Magazines like *Forbes* now tout the four hundred richest Americans. And a common question asked about people is, "How much do they make and how much are they worth?"

GOD WILL MEET YOUR NEEDS

Jesus warned clearly about this appraisal of a human life. "One's life," He said, "does not consist in the abundance of the things he possesses" (Luke 12:15). He knew that His followers were concerned about their material well-being, so He turned their attention away from the quest to build fortunes with these words:

> Do not store up for yourselves treasures on earth, where moth and rust destroy, and where thieves break in and steal. But store up for yourselves treasures in heaven, where moth and rust do not destroy, and where thieves do not break in and steal. For where your treasure is, there your heart will be also. . . . No one can serve two masters. . . . You cannot serve both God and Money. (Matthew 6:19–21, 24 NIV)

To those who were deeply worried about the daily survival of themselves and their families, He had a promise and a warning:

> Do not worry about your life, what you will eat or drink; or about your body, what you will wear. Is not life more important than food, and the body more important than clothes? Look at the birds of the air; they do not sow or reap or store away in barns, and yet your heavenly Father feeds them. Are you not much more valuable than they? Who of you by worrying can add a single hour to his life?
>
> And why do you worry about clothes? See how the lilies of the field grow. They do not labor or spin. Yet I tell you that not even

Solomon in all his splendor was dressed like one of these. If that is how God clothes the grass of the field, which is here today and tomorrow is thrown into the fire, will he not much more clothe you, O you of little faith? So do not worry, saying, 'What shall we eat?' or 'What shall we drink?' or 'What shall we wear?' For the pagans run after all these things, and your heavenly Father knows that you need them. *But seek first his kingdom and his righteousness, and all these things will be given to you as well.* (Matthew 6:25–33 NIV; emphasis added)

God is fully aware of our material needs. He is aware of the needs of the poor beggar. He is aware of the needs of the corporate CEO seeking capital to build a factory or buy an overseas company. He can cause what we need to materialize as if out of nowhere. The same word of faith that can move a mountain can also move a mountain of debt or bring a mountain of money our way for the fulfillment of God's plans for us.

The quest in our life must be the kingdom of God and His righteousness, not money. If we constantly seek money, it seems to elude us. If money becomes our god, then the loving Father will often move heaven and earth to keep it out of our way. With money as our god, we become doomed to tension, frustration, soul-wrenching disappointments, and ultimately a lonely, broken life. How many lives in our modern world have been shipwrecked because of the ethical corners that were cut in the pursuit of more and more money?

The answer is found in your priorities. If God and His righteousness are your goals—if you seek them first, as Jesus said—then God will silently, often miraculously, bring you more money than you believed was possible from sources of which you could not conceive.

The key is faith and trust. God is able to meet all of your needs "according to His riches in glory" (Philippians 4:19). God knows your needs down to the last penny. If you follow His plan and believe His promises, God intends to meet your needs. So, Jesus says to us, don't have the same priorities that the unbelievers have—stop worrying! It does you absolutely no good. Trust God and watch His provisions unfold for all of your material needs, great and small.

The next story is of a miracle of material provision that was frankly overwhelming.

GOD HAS POWER TO DO WHAT HE PROMISES

CBN, like most fast-growing small companies, was chronically short of funds. Bills would pile up and then get paid late. More explosive growth led to more bills and more need for additional money.

One day, about ten years after our founding as a company, the finance people came to me and said, "We have to have $1.5 million to make critical payments to our vendors." I reminded them that I wasn't God, nor was I the Federal Reserve Board. I had no power to print money, and they knew it. But since I was the company president, it was my job to find the money to pay our bills. The problem was, I didn't have the money we needed, CBN didn't have the money we needed, and, frankly, I had no idea where we could get it.

I carried that burden home for the night. The next morning, I brought the problem before the Lord and asked for His solution. I opened the Bible to the fourth chapter of Paul's letter to the Romans, where the apostle laid out clearly the incredible faith that had motivated the patriarch Abraham, who had been promised by God a great miracle. Abraham, at one hundred years of age (and with no heir), and Sarah, his ninety-year-old barren wife, were to conceive a son. God promised that their progeny would be as numerous as the grains of sand on the seashore and the stars and that through Abraham's "seed," all the nations of the world would be blessed (see Genesis 22:17–18).

It was an impossible dream. It was a promise that defied logic. It required not only a miracle in Abraham and Sarah's lives; it required successive miracles into the distant future. It required Abraham to look beyond the decades during which he and Sarah unsuccessfully tried to conceive a child and to believe that Sarah, at age ninety, could possibly get pregnant with a child.

As the apostle Paul states the matter:

> In the sight of God, in whom he believed—the God who gives life to the dead and calls things that are not as though they were. Against all hope, Abraham in hope believed and so became the father of many nations. . . . Without weakening in his faith, he faced the fact that his body was as good as dead—since he was about a hundred years old—and that Sarah's womb was also dead. Yet he did not waver through unbelief regarding the promise of God, but was strengthened in his faith and gave glory to God, *being fully persuaded that God had power to do what he had promised.* (Romans 4:17–21 NIV; emphasis added)

I read that line again: ". . . being fully persuaded that God had power to do what he had promised."

Then I read it again: ". . . being fully persuaded that God had power to do what he had promised."

Then I read it again: ". . . being fully persuaded that God had power to do what he had promised."

Then I read it again, and I read it yet again.

When I had finished, I was fully persuaded that God had power to do what He had promised. God had promised the future for CBN. He had called me to "claim the airways." He had not called me to be consumed by a hurricane, and He had not called me to be consumed by unpaid bills. I felt faith rising in my heart. I had not the slightest clue how God was going to provide the urgently needed $1.5 million, but I was "fully persuaded" that He was going to provide it.

The answer came within hours, and I still stand in joyous amazement at what happened.

My office was located in a rented floor of an office building about an hour's drive from where I lived. As I made the drive, I was pondering the problem and relying on God's solution.

When I sat down at my desk, my secretary came in holding a shoebox wrapped in brown paper. "Look what came in the mail today!" she exclaimed. The package was from a woman I did not know from a small town with which I was not familiar. When I lifted the lid on the shoebox, I discovered that the box was crammed full of bonds—New York state bearer bonds. The bonds added all together had a face value of $600,000 and a market value of $500,000!

I was holding in my hands the largest gift in CBN's history, which had just appeared unsolicited from a woman I had never heard of before. A shoebox—wrapped in brown wrapping paper and sent through the mail—with a half-million dollars worth of negotiable securities!

But this was just the beginning.

I went next-door to a small conference room to meet with the bookkeeping folks. No sooner had I sat down than my secretary came in with a letter in her hand. "Look what just came in!" She laughed and then handed the envelope to me. In it was a ticket to the New York state lottery, along with a letter explaining that this was the winning ticket for a one-million-dollar lottery prize. The owner wanted to give the winning ticket to CBN!

One million dollars—sent through the mail, unsolicited—from a person we did not know and had never heard of before!

It was as if God had smiled down and said, "Do you see how easy it is for Me to provide for your needs? Just two pieces of mail sent on one day, and your needs are met."

I can testify to what happened because I was there. The Bible is absolutely true. If we seek first the kingdom of God and His righteousness, all these material things will be added unto us. And if you hadn't guessed it already, many years later I am still "fully persuaded that God had power to do what he had promised."

(In the interest of full disclosure, the New York lottery ticket later proved to be good, but for less prize money than the donor thought he was giving. However, the Lord quickly made up the difference from more traditional sources, and CBN's bills were all paid.)

Gold and silver, oil and gas, precious jewels, real estate—these were all made from nothing by the word of God. The writer of the Book of Hebrews tells us, "By faith we understand that the universe was formed at God's command, so that what is seen was not made out of what was visible" (11:3 NIV).

Perhaps one of the reasons that Jesus had such disdain for the accumulation of material wealth was because He knew that God could create unlimited wealth merely with a word. By a word He could bring water out of a rock in the desert (Numbers 20:11), and He could by a word cause food to multiply in sufficient quantity to feed a multitude (Matthew 14:21).

GOD'S POWER OVER THE MATERIAL WORLD

During the brief period of Jesus's ministry, large crowds followed Him wherever He went. On one occasion, news reached Him of the tragic beheading of John the Baptist at the hands of King Herod. As a result, He wanted privacy to pray and to grieve. But privacy was denied Him, because even though He took a boat "to a solitary place" (Matthew 14:13 NIV), the crowd followed around the lake on foot.

According to the account in the fourteenth chapter of Matthew's Gospel, five thousand people were crowding around Him as evening approached. Jesus's disciples said, "This is a remote place, and it's already getting late. Send the crowds away, so they can go to the villages and buy themselves some food."

Jesus calmly replied, "They do not need to go away. You give them something to eat" (vv. 15–16 NIV).

Of course, to the disciples, this was an impossible task. How could they possibly feed all those people? There was no bread. No meat. No kitchens in which to cook. The hungry crowd was quite large: five thousand men, plus women and children.

But Jesus wanted His disciples to learn God's power over the material world. He wanted a miracle to take place—not in His hands, but in theirs. They were going to perform a miracle that evening in that remote place where no human intervention was possible.

Then He illustrated a key principle in God's economic plan: He begins with what you have. In the case of Moses, it was a long stick. With a stick, God would defeat the most powerful nation on earth. In the case of the hungry crowd near the Sea of Galilee, it was a little boy's lunch— five flat, round cakes of what we would call pita bread and two small fish.

Jesus took this tiny bit of food, and He blessed it. He knew that the same God who created matter in the first place had the power to multiply the matter that was in His hands. Jesus looked up to heaven, prayed a prayer of thanks, and broke the bread. He handed the pieces to His disciples to give to the crowd now sitting on the grass in front of Him.

Bread for Each Day

Imagine what was going on in the minds of the disciples. Here were all those hungry people. The disciples held in their hands portions of bread and fish, good enough for a snack for one, maybe two people. Were they fearful of failure? Were their spirits filled with supernatural faith? Were they blindly obedient to the command of Jesus? The Bible is silent on this. Nevertheless, each disciple went out into the crowd and broke off some food and gave it out. To His amazement, the bread and fish grew back. He then broke off some more and gave it away. Immediately, the bread and fish grew back. Time and again this happened until every man, woman, and child had received all they desired to eat.

Again, we have demonstrated the miracle principle. Faith comes from a word of God. Faith then prompts some human action. That action triggers the mighty response of God that we call a miracle. Faith ignores the impossibility of the task but focuses solely on the word of God.

The same God who restored Marlene Klepees's body, the same God who restored life and health into the dead body of Connie Davis, the same God who stopped a hurricane is the God who can cause bread to multiply to feed a multitude.

"HEY, GOD! YOU PROMISED!"

I love the childlike faith of some of the Italian immigrants who came to America, met Jesus Christ, and were then filled with God's Holy Spirit. To them, if it is in the Bible, it is true. To them, whatever God has promised in the Bible, He will do!

The mother of my friend, the late Frank Foglio, came to America without much money, but with a ton of faith. Frank wrote a wonderful book about his amazing mother entitled *Hey God!* (Bridge-Logos, 1972), and this is one story from it.

Italian people are very hospitable. The women are renowned cooks who delight in serving delicious food to their guests. Mama Foglio found herself one day with a crowd of guests at lunchtime. But what could she do? The family was poor, and her food supply had diminished to a half box of spaghetti. But Mama Foglio knew her Bible, and she knew the God of miracles.

So she got out her biggest pot, filled it with water, and then put it on the stove to boil. She took the tiny bit of uncooked spaghetti and put it near the pot. She then opened her Bible to a promise of God's provision and held it up in her right hand.

In a prayer that I am sure must have delighted the Lord, but which would have horrified most formal clergymen, Mama Foglio placed her finger on the promise in the Bible held in her uplifted hand and shouted at the top of her lungs, "Hey, God! You promised right here to meet my needs. I need food for all these people. Do it, God, just like You promised!"

She took the handful of spaghetti and threw it in the pot of boiling water. Before her eyes, the spaghetti began to swell until it filled up the giant container. When it was cooked, she served plate after plate of steaming delicious spaghetti so that all of her guests were fed.

Mama Foglio's prayer wasn't fancy. It wasn't couched in the old English of the King James Bible. But to the Foglio family, "Hey, God! Look! Right here You promised!" seemed prayer enough to please God and bring forth a miracle of multiplication and provision.

GOD'S PROVISION IS BEYOND WHAT WE CAN IMAGINE

Jesus tells us that our heavenly Father knows our need before we ask Him, so our constant petitions for financial success may be missing the mark. In fact, in one case of financial need, the Lord stopped me from praying for money to meet the need. Here is what happened.

Bread for Each Day

The Channel 27 studio building that I had acquired from Tim Bright was good enough for a start, but in truth, it was woefully inadequate. The southwest corner of the building—nearer the water—had been settling. It started to look like a wedge had broken off from a cake. We had three small offices and a small reception area. One local newspaper columnist described the studio as "slightly bigger than an executive cloakroom." Nothing was adequate to accommodate our growth. We praised God for what we had and did not "despise the day of small things" (Zechariah 4:10). Nevertheless, it was clear that we needed larger quarters.

I commissioned an architect to draw up a plan that enabled us to keep broadcasting where we were while we added an extension to the building and then bridged over the entire ground level with a much-needed second story. We endured dust, mud, rain, leaky roofs, and the construction racket for about a year. Finally, the beautiful new structure was finished. The general contractor proudly announced the news and handed me a final bill for $200,000.

If you have read this far, you probably can guess what comes next. We were short the $200,000, so it was time to turn to our Source for help.

Our new second-floor offices were arranged in a U-shape, two on each of the three sides. At the heart of the U was an open area with windows, which was large enough to hold five or six workstations. Every day at noon was prayer time, and the inaugural day of our new offices was no exception. We met at noon on this day for prayer. We were kneeling around chairs in the office open area. Some prayed silently, some out loud.

The cry arising from my heart was for the Lord to supply the money needed to finish paying for the construction—$200,000. As I was praying with great intensity, the Lord spoke to me: "Don't pray for the money! I want you to pray for the world." When He said that, I received what could only be described as a waking vision. In my mind's eye, I saw Jesus holding in His hands a globe—the entire world. Then as I looked, He opened my heart and placed the globe inside my heart.

That moment transformed me. Up to that time for the past nine years my focus—my passion—had been directed toward keeping one television station, WYAH-TV, and its companion radio station, WXRI-FM, on the air and ever improving. America, primarily the East Coast of America, had demanded my attention. Now God was saying to me what He said to John Wesley centuries before: "The world is your parish."

It was not long after this transforming experience that a chance arose to begin broadcasting on radio in Bogotá, Columbia.

Some time later, we began to air the *700 Club* television program each weekday on the GMA 7 national network in the Philippines. We became the first United States ministry in history to broadcast a daily television program overseas. Then followed regular television programs in Chile, Peru, El Salvador, Guatemala, Panama, the Dominican Republic, Costa Rica, Brazil, and Japan. As the years went by, there were regular television broadcasts in the former Soviet Union and the East Bloc countries, all over Africa, Indonesia, India, China, Southeast Asia, and the Middle East.

At this writing, thirty-seven years after God spoke to me to "pray for the world," CBN has television studios in Jakarta, Indonesia; Hyderabad, India; Kiev in the Ukraine; and Manila in the Philippines. Our programs are seen in some two hundred countries using more than thirty different languages. To date, our surveys show us that since the fall of Communism in the Soviet Union, an amazing 369 million people in all those nations have prayed with the host of one or more of our programs to receive Jesus Christ as their Lord and Savior.

By the way, I should add that as we were obedient to the Lord's call to pray for the world, He quickly paid off the $200,000 bill from our building contractor! What Jesus said is true: "Seek first the kingdom of God and His righteousness, and all these things shall be added to you" (Matthew 6:33).

A NETWORK IS BORN

During our early decades, we added owned and operated television stations in Atlanta, Dallas, and Boston. We had perfected the technique of videotaping segments of our program each day, and then airing two, three, or even four hours a day on commercial affiliate stations. What had been called in faith the Christian Broadcasting Network was, in reality, becoming just that—a network. Our television programs were reaching across the United States to major markets, such as Charlotte, Visalia, Chicago, Houston, Baltimore, Washington, Seattle, New York, Los Angeles, Sacramento, and dozens of others. Rapid expansion brought great ministry opportunities, as well as great financial obligations.

In 1973, two wonderful things happened. We went to Houston, Texas, for a weekend fundraising telethon at our affiliate station Channel 26. It was a time I will never forget. At four o'clock on a Friday afternoon when our telethon began, I opened with an invitation for the audience to receive Christ. There were fifty-five telephones in the studio that were sitting quietly on desks when I began. After the invitation, a veritable explosion of calls began. Every phone rang. And they rang and rang and rang without ceasing until we signed off at two o'clock the next morning. Hundreds and ultimately thousands of people called to say that they had been born again—or that they had been healed—or that they wanted prayer. We were supposed to be raising money to pay the costs of operating in Houston. The money we needed came in, but it was clearly secondary to the spiritual revival that was taking place.

Our team flew from Houston to Dallas, where we were putting on the air a newly owned and operated station, KXTX-TV, on Channel 33. Our initial thinking was that since Dallas was a large and sophisticated city, we should tone down some of our more exuberant demonstrations of God's power. Our new station carried a full lineup of children's programs, situation comedies, Western series like *Bonanza*, and wholesome movies aimed at a general family audience.

We had reserved key prime time for ministry on our *700 Club* program. On the first program day in Dallas, the *700 Club* program originated live from the KXTX studio. When the time came to pray, God moved in, and all our cautious reserve was thrown away. Extraordinary miracles took place in Dallas that day.

There is one that stands out vividly. As I prayed, I sensed the Holy Spirit saying that there was someone in the audience with an ugly infected "gash" all around her back, and it was being healed. To my delight, a telephone call came in after a short while to our Dallas telephone counselors from a woman in Ardmore, Oklahoma. This woman had been operated on for a kidney problem, but the incision across her back had become infected, red, and was draining pus. She was sitting on a piano stool watching television when my word of knowledge was spoken.

God's power was so strong through the television set that she was literally knocked to the floor. When she came to, her "gash" was healed, and she was rejoicing in the Lord. In the next chapter, I will be presenting for you several other instances when Almighty God reached down and performed miracles in the lives of those who were hopelessly ill.

Our spiritual successes were overwhelming. In a short twelve years, God was bringing about a fulfillment of His word in a manner beyond anything I could have asked or dreamed. We knew that much greater things were ahead.

But one thing constantly gnawed at us—lack of money. God was blessing us wonderfully spiritually, but we were constantly behind financially. What could we do? What was God's way to regular financial blessing?

Our small board of directors had come to Dallas for the opening of our new television station, so we held a board meeting at the Adolphus Hotel in downtown Dallas. We prayed at length, considered our cash shortfalls, and then, with complete unity and joy of heart, made a decision that forever changed our financial situation.

We all knew what the Bible said about giving. Jesus said, "Give, and it will be given to you. A good measure, pressed down, shaken together and running over will be poured into your lap" (Luke 6:38 NIV). We were aware of the eternal promise found in the book of the prophet Malachi, who, speaking on behalf of the Lord, boldly declared, "'Test me in this [tithes and offerings],' says the LORD Almighty, 'and see if I will not throw open the floodgates of heaven and pour out so much blessing that you will not have room enough for it'" (3:10 NIV).

To be sure, CBN was a nonprofit ministry, but weren't we also under the eternal laws of giving and receiving? How could we speak a command to money if the precondition for the answer had not been met? Here again, faith goes against logic. Logic says, "Wait until you have surpluses before you give." God says, "Test Me by your giving, and then I will pour out surpluses for you."

Our board unanimously agreed. We would lay aside human logic and go the route of faith. Despite budget shortfalls, we would tithe our income to other ministries, to missions, and to the poor. We all knew that this was the right course. Painful as it may have seemed to our accounting staff, we realized that God was leading us into financial blessing through obedience. The Lord had promised us that if we were faithful to tithe, He would open the floodgates (the windows) of heaven and pour out such a blessing that we could not contain.

He keeps His word. In 1986, just thirteen years after our step of faith, I was able to calculate the amount of our giving. Our tithe alone that year was almost five times our *total income* in 1973. Not five times our 1973 "tithe." The "tithe," the amount our increased income allowed us to give away, was five times the amount of *all of our 1973 income!* God waits for people to discover His secrets and then, through these secrets, move on to miracles that can seem unimaginable.

When good seed is planted by God's direction, that plant will keep on growing if it is nourished by prayer, faith, and obedience. CBN was God's planting, and its growth at home and abroad has been dramatic. We outgrew our remodeled building. Then we added a lean-to stage prop facility in the back. We installed two house trailers for offices. We then bought two old houses next-door for more offices. We rented a warehouse office facility in an adjoining city for our mail processing. Then we rented an office suite in a downtown Portsmouth bank building for the accountants. Finally, we moved most of our executive offices to an entire floor of an office building in the Pembroke area at the center of the city of Virginia Beach.

I am convinced that in God's economy, we must use to the fullest what He has given us before He gives us more. Faith has a way of arising out of necessity—even out of desperation—rather than out of a wish list of our human desires. Without question, CBN was using every square inch of our facility to its maximum, and our crazy quilt pattern of temporary housing violated the basic principles of sound management and corporate communication. Yet God's plan for us was much bigger than what we had attained, and none of what we had in 1974 would even come close to accommodating our future.

So I began looking for land on which to build a good-sized building to house offices, studios, control rooms, and a counseling center. The corner lot next to our Pembroke office was vacant, but not for sale. A vacant two- to three-acre lot several miles away was used to store construction machinery, but the owner refused all entreaties to sell. Finally, the Virginia Beach City Development Department suggested that we might be able to buy six acres from a group of developers who had assembled a 143-acre shopping center/office park site called Metroplex, just off the only interstate highway exit in the city.

I asked the owners about the possibility of purchasing six acres on the edge of their property. The answer—a firm no!

Christians must realize that God will, if they don't fight Him, continually say no to second best until His time comes to give us the very best. I was trying to be conservative and practical in my thinking. I kept pushing on the doors that would lead to second best. God made sure that those doors were slammed in my face.

In truth, God had planned a place for us since the founding of America. He had kept it safe from intruders. He had surrounded it with wonderful highways. He made it big enough to accommodate something else that He had in mind, which He had not yet revealed to me. I thought I was being stymied by narrow-minded landholders. In truth, I was standing on the edge of a great adventure that would catapult us into a whole new dimension of ministry.

Pastor Ralph Wilkerson had acquired a Southern California entertainment complex called Melodyland, which was located across a broad boulevard from the world-famous Disneyland. Ralph had built a dynamic church called Melodyland Christian Center. After a few years, he added Melodyland School of Theology. Ralph asked me to join the board of trustees of the school, and I accepted.

In the early fall of 1975, I took time off from my property search in order to fly to Anaheim, California, for the board meeting of the school. The first meeting was a luncheon held in the penthouse dining room of the Grand Hotel across from Disneyland.

I arrived quite late to the luncheon and was unwilling to break into an event long in progress. So I ducked into the modest coffee shop off the hotel lobby and ordered for my lunch a half of a cantaloupe filled with cottage cheese. When my modest lunch arrived, I bowed my head to say grace.

Then it happened. God began speaking to me with great clarity: "Don't try to buy six acres. Buy the entire tract of land. Build your headquarters, and build a school for My glory!"

I was stunned. A school! What kind of school? I had never started a school. I had never run a school. Yet God had clearly spoken, and His faith in me now rose to do what He said. God had a great miracle of provision in store.

I flew back to Virginia and called John Zimmerman, who was an executive vice president of the bank that held a foreclosed mortgage on the Metroplex property. After a few words of greeting, I began. "I have just come back from California. The Lord has told me not to try to buy six acres, but to buy the entire Metroplex tract to build our headquarters and a school for His glory."

Without hesitation, this brilliant banker, who obviously wanted to clear foreclosed property off of the bank's books, almost shouted, "Praise the Lord!"

"How do you want to pay for it?" he asked.

With the boldness of faith, I replied, "Nothing down, interest only for two years, and the balance in equal payments over the next twenty-three years."

Without any hesitation, he came back, "What interest will you pay?"

"Eight percent simple," I answered.

"I think we can do it," he replied. "I will have our lawyers draw up the papers."

I thanked him and hung up the phone. God had just handed us one of the finest locations in our entire multicity area for nothing down and a painless long-term payout. It was a miracle. It was quick. It was easy. It was God's perfect plan for us!

On December 31, 1975, my wife and I, on behalf of the Christian Broadcasting Network, took title to an absolutely beautiful wooded tract located at the corner of a road that was later broadened to eight lanes, with an exit on Interstate 64, which is the arterial loop for all of the Tidewater cities. Our land borders Virginia Beach, Norfolk, and Chesapeake. On January 1, 1976, our staff walked the outer boundary of the land and dedicated it to the glory of the Lord. He gave it to us and we, in prayer, gave it back to Him.

For those of you who may be interested in finance, I am happy to report that this land, which cost $2.3 million on easy terms for 143 acres, is now valued at approximately $400,000 per acre—a total of $57.2 million. And as some people would call "serendipity," over the next several years, the Lord enabled me to acquire adjoining parcels of land until we had 700 acres and two full miles of frontage on the interstate.

In subsequent decades, our extra 500 acres has been considered the largest contiguous piece of undeveloped commercial land in the entire city, and the price of the "extra land" has risen to about $300,000 an acre. After waiting a number of years, we have decided to lease out the land for a town center and mixed-use commercial and residential construction.

When hundreds of millions of dollars of construction is finished on land that we have leased to tenants, CBN will then have a sizeable endowment to assist it in its worldwide ministry in the decades to come.

It's easy to see now what I didn't see in the early days . . . that God had blessings for us beyond what we could ask or think. I shudder at the thought that God's vision would have been cramped into a two- to three-acre parcel next to an office building in Virginia Beach. The message is clear: "Wait on the LORD. . . . Wait, I say, on the LORD!" (Psalm 27:14).

BUILDING A SCHOOL FOR GOD'S GLORY

But what of the school that I was to build for His glory? I pondered the problem and asked for the Lord's leading. Finally in the summer of 1977, the answer came one afternoon in Kansas City where we had journeyed to produce our television program, the *700 Club*, in conjunction with the annual convention of the Christian Booksellers' Association.

During a brief break as I sat by the motel pool, the plan emerged. There was to be a university to challenge the culture in television, film, journalism, law, government, education, business, and divinity. It was to be a unique institution with freestanding graduate schools made up of mature Christians who were seeking to acquire the skills needed to take a leadership role in society. There would be no athletic teams, no gyms, no stadium, no fraternities, no childish pranks. This was graduate education with the motto: Christian Leadership to Change the World.

With key advice from a lawyer friend, I drafted the articles of incorporation of "CBN University" and sent them in to the Secretary of State of Virginia. A couple of weeks later, the Lord's university received official status.

In September 1978, after we had recruited seven brave professors and seventy-seven equally brave students, we opened the Communications

School of CBN University to offer a master of arts degree in radio, television, and film.

The miracle story of CBN University, which later became Regent University, could fill a volume in itself. The students at Regent are extraordinary. The school can now boast of ten thousand alumni, and a current student body of forty-six hundred. Our law students' moot court team beat Yale in national competition; one of our students wrote the best moot court brief in the nation; one of our education school graduates was voted the best middle school principal in the nation; our film students have won 133 national and regional film awards, including an Oscar as the best college film of the year; one of our students, Nicole Johnson, was chosen as Miss America; our law and government students are working in important positions in the government and a number have won elections; one of our business school grads was chosen as eBay retailer of the year; our doctoral students now hold teaching positions in higher education across America; enrollment at our graduate school of divinity places it in the top ten of the nation's theological schools; and Regent's endowment is currently the largest of any evangelical institution in the United States.

The Lord breathed the command over a simple luncheon of cantaloupe and cottage cheese: "Buy all the land. Build your headquarters and build a school for My glory." Each day as I look around the beautiful Georgian-style campus of CBN and Regent University, I see before me the miracle power of a God who calls into being what is from what is not . . . who makes what is seen from what was not visible.

HE HEALS THE SICK

As I write this book, television, newspapers, and magazines are daily headlining alarming stories of an impending pandemic of avian flu, otherwise known as bird flu. This dreaded killer seems to fly with the wind. It was first seen in Hong Kong and Shanghai, then Thailand, and soon after in Russia and Europe. First carried from domestic fowl to migrating birds, the virus is expected to slowly, inexorably mutate from its deadly work among birds to even more deadly work among human beings. Infectious disease specialists tell us that the World War I–era flu pandemic that took the lives of millions was also a strain of bird flu. They also tell us that no available vaccine will be available to combat this menace until the virus has successfully mutated to its final form as a killer of people.

But bird flu is not the only disease facing mankind. Three hundred million people in the Third World are suffering the debilitating chills, fever, and lethargy of mosquito-borne malaria. HIV/AIDS is spreading with alarming rapidity. In some African nations, close to 50 percent of the population is infected with the disease, and there are now more than ten million orphans in Africa whose parents died of AIDS.

Healthcare costs in the United States will consume close to 15 percent of the total economic output of the nation. Obesity is epidemic, along with high blood pressure, heart attacks, stroke, cancer, and diabetes.

Whether it is caused by lifestyle choices, parasites carried in polluted water, bloodsucking insects, or a respiratory virus carried by birds, a wave of sickness has been darkening the face of our globe. If ever there was a time for Christians to lay claim to the miraculous healing power of Jesus Christ, it is now.

The Bible makes it clear—in fact, it almost takes for granted—that the disciples of Jesus would heal the sick. When Jesus sent out seventy-two of His disciples throughout Judea, He gave them this command: "When you enter a town and are welcomed, eat what is set before you. *Heal the sick who are there* and tell them, 'The kingdom of God is near you'" (Luke 10:8–9 NIV; emphasis added).

In the Gospel of Matthew, we read of twelve disciples who came to Jesus, and He "gave them authority to drive out evil spirits and to heal every disease and sickness" (10:1 NIV). He specifically instructed them, "As you go, preach this message: 'The kingdom of heaven is near.' *Heal the sick*, raise the dead, cleanse those who have leprosy, drive out demons. Freely you have received, freely give" (vv. 7–8 NIV; emphasis added).

The first chapter of the Gospel of Mark records one day in the life of Jesus after He returned to Galilee. It was the Sabbath, so He went to the synagogue in Capernaum. While there, He cast a demon out of a demon-possessed man. From the synagogue, He went to the home of Simon and Andrew. He found Simon Peter's mother-in-law in bed with a fever, and He immediately healed her. The chapter goes on to say, "That evening after sunset the people brought to Jesus all the sick and demon-possessed. The whole town gathered at the door, and Jesus healed many who had various diseases. He also drove out many demons" (Mark 1:32–34 NIV).

He Heals the Sick

Shortly afterward, as He traveled around Galilee, a man with leprosy knelt before Him and begged Him for healing, saying, "If you are willing, you can make me clean."

Jesus's response was to touch the man and utter these words: "'I am willing. Be clean!' Immediately the leprosy left him and he was cured" (vv. 40–42 NIV).

SOURCES OF SICKNESS

Through the years, many well-meaning Christians assert with great earnestness that it is not "God's will" to heal people. To them I reply, "Jesus Christ is the perfect, sinless human being who always did what pleased the Father. In the entire biblical record, there is not, to the best of my knowledge, one single instance in which Jesus Christ refused physical healing to anyone. If He was the perfect expression of the Father's will, then we must conclude that physical healing through prayer is clearly in the Father's will."

Jesus looked with compassion at a suffering leper who had raised that very question, and then with great earnestness He said, "I am willing. Be clean!" (Mark 1:41 NIV).

Then there are those who are persuaded that sickness is a curse from God. I will say beyond any doubt that lifestyle decisions can cause ill health. Cigarette smoking can cause lung cancer and emphysema. Eating high-glycemic carbohydrates like cakes, pies, cookies, and white bread can cause diabetes, high blood pressure, strokes, and heart attacks. Consumption of alcoholic beverages can kill brain cells, which leads to diminished cognition and senile dementia.

Failure to nourish the body with adequate vitamins and minerals can lead to a host of cardiovascular problems, the breakdown of cells, lowered immune system, free radical damage, and susceptibility to a host of viral infections, premature aging, and cancer.

Emotional stress is a great killer, as is guilt, shame, fear, and grief. Hatred and bitterness—lack of forgiveness—can lead to a host of psychosomatic or soul-body diseases including arthritis or even paralysis. Exhaustion, extreme exposure to cold, and trauma lead to countless sicknesses. And demons can bring about a host of infirmities that we classify as sickness.

In short, as Psalm 139:14 tells us, we are "fearfully and wonderfully made." Our physical well-being is affected by myriad factors—some outside of us, some inside of us.

Jesus had perfect understanding of the source of problems confronting those people who needed help. A paralytic man was brought to Him lying on a pallet. Jesus did not say to him immediately, "Get up." Instead, He said, "Son, your sins are forgiven" (Mark 2:5 NIV). Only later, as a demonstration to His critics, did He tell the paralytic, "Get up, take your mat and go home" (v. 11 NIV).

To a crippled man lying by the pool of Bethesda, Jesus asked, "Do you want to get well?" (John 5:6 NIV). Somehow, He realized that the cripple had given up. He first needed to stand up inside by faith before he could stand up physically. He had to stop using his illness as an excuse for failure and determine that indeed he wanted to be healed of his malady.

To a boy who was evidencing signs of epilepsy, Jesus did not speak of healing. Instead, He identified the demon that was causing the problem and cast it forth (Matthew 17:18).

Jesus clearly knew which illness was caused by sin (Mark 2:5); which illness was caused by psychological causes (John 5:6); and which illness was caused by demons (Matthew 17:18). He also knew when congenital blindness was caused neither by sins of the parents or by the sins of the individual, but for the glory of God (John 9:2–3). And He knew when a woman seeking healing for a loved one needed to be pushed harder so that strong faith would emerge (Matthew 15:23–28).

MODERN MEDICINE AND THE POWER OF GOD

It is clear that Jesus Christ did not live in a time of modern medicine. In His day, if a man developed cataracts, he needed a divine miracle to save him from eventual blindness. If there was paralysis or trauma, either a divine miracle occurred or the person became a helpless cripple. If there was a birth defect such as a cleft palate or crossed eyes, there was no readily available surgery to correct the problem and bring about a normal appearance. Either God performed a miracle, or the individual went through life disfigured.

It is clear why the people mobbed Jesus. He brought them relief from their suffering that they could obtain nowhere else. In desperation, their faith reached out to the only source available for healing—Almighty God.

In our modern world, this is not the case. Why should we agonize in prayer for a healing of a headache when a bottle of cheap painkillers is in our medicine cabinet? Why ask for a miracle when a prescription drug or simple surgery can alleviate our suffering? As a result, many people grow totally dependent on doctors and modern medicine. And when modern medicine gives up hope, then they feel doomed.

I believe that modern medicine is a gift of God. Several years ago, CBN purchased a Lockheed 1011 large jet airliner, then had it completely outfitted as an ultramodern flying hospital. With a full complement of Christian doctors and nurses and a cargo hold full of medicine, we brought this angel of mercy to India, Brazil, Kazakhstan, the Ukraine, Ecuador, El Salvador, Guatemala, Mexico, and other desperately poor regions. Thousands of the poor who could not afford medical treatment lined up for help. Our doctors performed eye surgery, removed skin cancers, extracted embedded bullets, rendered transforming plastic surgery, removed life-threatening spinal tumors, performed a hip replacement, and dispensed thousands of doses of critically needed antibiotics, as well as thousands of pairs of free eyeglasses.

Overall, the Flying Hospital and other smaller medical teams from CBN and its sister organization, Operation Blessing, have so far treated about 1.8 million poor patients around the world. We did this in the name of Jesus because He cares for those who suffer.

We believe in medicine and in bringing the best of advanced medical technology to alleviate the suffering of the poor. However, we know that God Almighty also intervenes today to provide healing miracles to suffering people. In fact, noted pollster George Gallup Jr. told me more than twenty years ago that his surveys in the United States revealed that an astounding 7.5 million people reported having received a physical healing in answer to prayer.

There should be no conflict whatsoever between modern holistic medicine and the miracle power of God. God uses the skills of doctors and the marvels of modern medicine. God uses faith and prayer. Recent surveys report a direct correlation between prayer and healing from surgery or other sickness. Those who attend church and have strong faith have fewer illnesses and much shorter recovery times when they are sick than unbelievers and nonchurchgoers.

Leaving aside the miraculous, there is a clear correlation between our mental and spiritual state and the physical condition of our bodies. In fact, one Christian doctor told me that, in his opinion, 70 percent of non-drug-induced illness is psychosomatic. In other words, the body is suffering because the soul is suffering. The link between faith and medicine was clearly enunciated years ago by a man of medicine who said, "I bind the wound, but it is God who does the healing."

This book is about miracles. Since the inception of our ministry, CBN has received to the date of this writing some 70,720,000 calls for prayer, of which 14,900,000 have been for healing. Although there are many instances of answers to prayer of which we are not aware, we do know that over the years in excess of 1 million have reported wonderful, miraculous answers to prayer.

GOD'S POWER OVER SICKNESS

Let me tell you the story of Alan and Lisa Knupp, a mom and dad who were eyewitnesses to God's miraculous touch on their son Logan after doctors had given him only four months to live.

The Knupps were relishing all the joys of raising two little boys, three-year-old Tyler and eight-month-old Logan. Like all parents, they looked forward to watching their kids grow up to experience all the adventures life has to offer. And the young family was thoroughly involved in their church in southwestern Pennsylvania and growing in their faith in Christ.

But at eight months, Logan began displaying a few oddities in his behavior. He slept more than normal. When he should have been able to sit up on his own, he kept falling over. He developed lazy eye in both eyes, and he began projectile vomiting daily. After a thorough exam, an ophthalmologist ruled out a possible brain tumor. But Logan's parents felt uneasy about the continuing symptoms, so they scheduled a precautionary MRI. The MRI revealed that Logan did have a cancerous brain tumor at the top of his spine that required immediate surgery. Doctors told Alan and Lisa that their little boy was very sick and had only a 10 percent chance of reaching his first birthday.

Left alone with Logan in his hospital room after the MRI, Alan and Lisa were devastated, their dreams for Logan seemingly being ripped from them. Alan, who was suffering depression at that time from a very high-stress job, curled up on the floor of Logan's hospital room, moaning in grief. Lisa tried to comfort him, but she had her own dark fears to deal with.

As they waited in the dimly lit room for details of Logan's brain surgery the following day, the door opened. The figure in the doorway was a silhouette against the light streaming in from the hall. Preoccupied with their grief, the Knupps couldn't tell who it was. The sudden stranger announced, "You're going to see a miracle" and then left the room and closed the door. When they compared notes much later, the couple agreed that God had sent an angel to their room to tell them what He planned to do.

The next day, surgeons removed a golf-ball-sized tumor from Logan's brain. The diagnosis was a metastatic tumor known as a glioma. However, in the process, the doctors discovered that the tumor had spread. An MRI the next day revealed that the malignancy spanned the length of the infant's spinal cord. Not only was the tumor inoperable, but radiation therapy was impossible without damaging Logan's brain. Chemotherapy was the only option, but the prognosis for cure was slim to none.

Alan collapsed in the arms of family members when the prognosis was announced. "I thought it was the end," he says. "I thought it was just a matter of days until he died. I was wishing I could take his place because he was only a baby."

Lisa battled self-condemnation over Logan's illness. She felt responsible for what was happening to her son. She thought she had let Logan and everyone else down by genetically contributing to his illness. The doctors assured her that it was nothing she had done, that the cells in Logan's body just went crazy. It made sense, but Lisa still found it difficult to absolve herself of guilt for contributing to her son's condition.

Stunned with grief, Alan and Lisa made an important decision. The doctors offered little hope, but God's Word assured them that nothing was impossible. The Knupps decided that they would listen to and respect the input from Logan's medical team, but they would place their faith in hope on what God said above what the doctors were saying.

Three weeks after the tumor was removed, Logan began aggressive chemotherapy. Doctors didn't view the radical treatment as a cure. They hoped only to buy a few months of quality time for the Knupp family to be together before the tumor grew back and Logan would die. Alan and Lisa drew strength from the hundreds of people who were praying for them and Logan—friends, family members, church members, and even strangers.

An acquaintance of the family named Marty shared with the Knupps a vision God gave her during prayer that Logan's healing had been accomplished. "As I prayed, I was aware that God was severing this cancer," Marty states. "I saw the Lord lay an ax to the base of the cancer, and the tumor was totally destroyed."

The day after Marty's powerful prayer, one month after the initial diagnosis and surgery, Logan was to begin his second week of chemotherapy. Doctors performed another MRI on Logan to see if the tumor was growing back. Alan and Lisa had been informed that an aggressive tumor like Logan's sometimes keeps growing through chemo. Doctors didn't want to continue the treatments if they weren't working. The Knupps waited anxiously to learn what the doctors discovered.

The MRI technician, who was the first to see the results of the scan, couldn't believe her eyes, so she called in the radiologist on duty.

Together they compared Logan's original scan with the one just completed. The tumor clouding the first MRI was completely gone in the second scan! The oncologist was equally amazed. They all agreed that the results were incredible, nothing short of a miracle.

When Alan and Lisa heard the news, they were guardedly optimistic. Logan had only received one week of chemo, and they didn't want their hopes to soar if there might be a mistake in the scan. Doctors ordered a spinal tap to check for cancer at the cellular level. Not one single cell was cancerous. Logan was completely cancer-free! What's more, Alan's depression had begun to lift, beginning the night an angel appeared at Logan's door with news of a miracle.

Logan's doctors were at a loss to explain the abrupt disappearance of the tumor that had coated the boy's spinal cord. They urged the Knupps to continue the chemo for three years as a precaution. Alan and Lisa agreed to the treatment, but they knew that Almighty God was responsible for their miracle more than the powerful drugs administered by the doctors.

As I write this, Logan Knupp has been cancer-free for eight years. He's a completely normal boy who loves sports and music. Logan has heard his parents tell the story of his miracle many times. He sums it up this way: "I was sick a lot, and I used to be in the hospital a lot. But God healed me."

Lisa and Alan definitely believe in miracles. They realize Jesus walked the earth two thousand years ago, touched people with all kinds of problems, and graciously healed them. But they also know Jesus heals today. This grateful couple regard Logan's complete healing as a gracious gift to them from God, announced by an angel.

"Yes, I believe in miracles," Lisa says. "I have one who lives with me every day."

He Heals the Sick

WALKING AWAY FROM HER WHEELCHAIR

I have available to me from our years of broadcasting remarkable accounts of God's healing power, like the miracle that happened to Janice Pridgen.

When Janice Pridgen woke up one morning, the entire left side of her body was paralyzed, and her face was contorted as if she had suffered a stroke. After a series of tests, doctors diagnosed her with chronic progressive multiple sclerosis. Janice told her husband, Johnny, "You can leave, you know. You don't have to stay with a sick woman the rest of your life." Having been married almost thirty years, Johnny wasn't about to bail out on the love of his life.

Soon Janice was a paraplegic, unable to care for herself or control her bodily functions. Within four years, she was bedridden. She couldn't go anywhere without the aid of a wheelchair. Complications from MS included diabetes and high blood pressure. One year Janice spent a total of six months in the hospital, but her condition grew worse. Once she lapsed into a diabetic coma and almost died.

Johnny and Janice never stopped praying for healing. Many times they saw no results to their prayers, but they continued to believe that she would walk again someday. In the meantime, Janice and Johnny attended their local church whenever she was able.

On May 23, 2004, fourteen years after Janice contracted MS, the couple went to church as usual. It was like every other Sunday. Pastor David Hodge was preaching, and the Pridgens were enjoying the gospel message. Then something very different happened. Janice says, "God said, 'Get up. You're going to walk today on holy ground.'" The suddenness of God's good news was overwhelming. It was God's appointed time for healing Janice after all those years of suffering, waiting, and trusting.

Janice stood and began to take steps. At first she had to hold on to the pews for support. But soon she was walking on her own. She walked around the sanctuary three times that day. "You talk about setting a church on fire!" Johnny exclaims. "When she began to walk, the whole church began to shout and praise the Lord."

When they got home that day, Janice told Johnny to take the wheelchair to the barn. It hasn't been used since. Janice realizes that people don't walk away from their wheelchairs every day, but she rejoices that God put her back on her feet after fourteen years. Isaiah 53:5 has become real to her: "By His stripes we are healed." "You just keep on believing in that," she says.

God performed an awesome miracle for Janice Pridgen. It was His miracle-working power that strengthened her legs and allowed her to walk again. But she and Johnny were God's partners in healing through their prayers and faith.

GOD'S POWER OVER CANCER

Few words prompt greater terror in the human heart than *cancer*. Everyone knows someone who is afflicted with this terrible disease. But God still does miracles of healing, and cancer victims are no exception, as Victoria Justiniano will joyfully testify.

Victoria discovered a problem when she accidentally bit her tongue while eating and the wound never healed. It kept bleeding and bleeding. Soon she experienced other strange symptoms, such as swelling and painful blood clots. After several blood tests, the doctor told Victoria that she had leukemia and that 90 percent of her blood cells were malignant. After the shocking diagnosis, she prayed, "God, I'm in Your hands. You are the best doctor."

Immediate, aggressive chemotherapy took a toll on Victoria: loss of hair, nausea, coughing up blood. Her trust for healing was in the Lord, and she did everything she knew to do from Scripture to receive God's touch. Down deep, she knew that Satan was trying to take her out with this illness. She prayed that God would grant her the desire of her heart: to see her fourteen-year-old son grow up. Despite her anxiety, Victoria's confidence grew that God would hear and answer her prayer for healing.

Victoria went into remission three times but always relapsed, each episode leaving her weaker. The doctors held little hope for Victoria, but thanks to a word from God, her pastor had a different view. Pastor Rissi was getting ready to leave his office for the day when God spoke to him forcefully: "When you pray for Victoria, I will heal her." The pastor headed straight for the hospital.

When he arrived, Victoria's family was in mourning. She had been hemorrhaging, losing more blood than doctors could pump into her. Doctors didn't expect her to survive the night. Pastor Rissi went into Victoria's room, and she was awake. He told her what God had said to him. "I know," she said weakly. "I've been waiting for it." The pastor prayed a simple prayer for healing and then left the room to let her rest.

The next day, Victoria's family was there when she woke up. She sat up, announced that she was very hungry, and ordered a big breakfast. Her doctor examined her and said the leukemia was gone. When she saw him for the last time, Victoria said, "I love you so much, but I don't ever want to see you again." Her doctor still doesn't understand why she is still alive.

Victoria has been cancer-free now for more than sixteen years with no signs of relapse! She is grateful to tell others about her healing. "It was such a blessing for me just to know that God had healed me for a reason, so that I'll be able to testify of His wonders and mercy to others. Trust the Lord. I did, and God healed me."

RESTORED TO LIFE

When Jesus Christ lived on earth, He healed all those who came to Him. He did not argue fine points of religious doctrine. They had come to Him in faith—some were Jewish, some were not. As we saw in an earlier chapter, one with "great faith" was a Roman officer (Matthew 8:10). Another with "great faith" was a Gentile woman from Tyre (Matthew 15:28). We call her a "Syro-Phoenician." Clearly she was not Jewish.

God looked beyond religious labels in Jesus's time and, as the next story reveals, He looks beyond religious labels today. This is the story of a miracle that happened for a Muslim, Dr. Mustapha Khan.

It was August 1965, and Mustapha Khan, his wife Jackie, and their five children were driving home to Camden, New Jersey, in the family station wagon after their summer vacation at Niagara Falls. Jackie Khan was a Christian, but her husband had been raised in Trinidad as a devout Muslim, and he was raising their children to be Muslims. Mustapha did not believe that Jesus Christ was the resurrected Son of God. He viewed Jesus as another prophet on a par with Moses or Muhammad.

Suddenly, a car traveling in the other direction crossed the median, heading right for them. Mustapha had to make a split-second decision. He could swerve to the right and send the car over the side of a steep cliff, a fall that would certainly kill his entire family. Or he could hit the car of the wrong-way driver and hope for the best. He chose a head-on collision.

The front passenger side of the car took the brunt of the impact. This was before lifesaving airbags were invented and seatbelts were mandatory. Mustapha and the children sustained injuries, but they were all still conscious. Looking over at his wife, Mustapha knew immediately that she was dead. He pulled Jackie from the mangled station wagon and laid her on the grass beside the highway. She had no pulse, no respiration, and blood seeped from her mouth. Mustapha knelt over his wife, weeping and calling her name.

Motorists arriving on the scene stopped and offered to help. Mustapha said there was nothing more to be done, that his wife was already dead. Somebody produced a sheet and pulled it over the bloody, lifeless body. Yet Mustapha sensed something inside him that challenged his acceptance of his wife's death. As a physician, he was committed to fight for the lives of his patients even when it seemed hopeless. He could do no less for his own wife, though he expected the attempt to be futile.

His oldest child, Riccardo, was with him beside the body. "Ricky, go find my doctor's bag in the car and bring it to me," he ordered. As Ricky was searching for the bag, Mustapha prepared his other four children for the worst. As his tears flowed, he went to them and announced, "Your mother has gone to heaven." The children had seen her and knew their father was telling the truth.

When his son returned with the bag, Mustapha administered an injection of epinephrine in an attempt to stimulate heart activity. He coached Ricky on how to do heart massage and then began mouth-to-mouth resuscitation. Amazingly, after only a few minutes, Jackie began to breathe, and Mustapha felt a spark of hope. By that time an ambulance had arrived, and the family was transported to the hospital.

Jackie Khan's injuries were severe. She had suffered broken ribs, contusion of the lungs, bleeding in the thoracic cavity, and a fractured pelvis. Mustapha believed in heaven, and he believed Jackie would go to heaven if she did not survive her injuries. He desperately wanted her to live, so all through the first night, as Jackie's life hung in the balance, he prayed to any god or prophet who might be listening, including the Savior Jackie served.

Jackie remained comatose in intensive care for a couple of days. One day, the family came into her room and she was smiling. She didn't know how long she had been out or what had happened to her. Mustapha told her the story. He also admitted that he had prayed for her all through the first night.

Jackie remained in the hospital for a month. When she finally came home to her family, Mustapha firmly decided what their first outing would be. "The first place we'll go when we leave the house won't be to a ball game or to have dinner," he announced. "We'll go to church." As soon as Jackie was able, they attended St. Augustine Episcopal Church. The rector, Father McKay, was a very godly man. Referring to the Khans' accident during his sermon, he called Jackie's recovery a miracle of God.

It was a new thought for Mustapha, who had previously regarded miracles only as huge religious events, such as the miracles of Lourdes, France. As he thought about it, Mustapha agreed that the God of the Christians had performed a miracle. His wife was dead, and now she was alive. Mustapha continued to take his family to a Christian church, but he was not about to give up his faith as a Muslim to become a Christian.

The power of God and the faith of his praying wife eventually changed his mind. Continuing his medical practice, Mustapha began praying to God in the name of Jesus Christ for miracles in the lives of his patients. Many of them experienced remarkable recoveries, and Mustapha was deeply touched. One by one over the years, each of the couple's four sons, Riccardo, Rasheed, Amir, and young Mustapha, as well as their daughter, Sherena, gave their hearts to Jesus. As an eyewitness to the growing, fervent Christian faith of his family, Mustapha finally bowed to Jesus Christ as Lord. He claims that Jackie had the greatest influence in his coming to faith in Christ.

He Heals the Sick

Now, more than forty years after the accident, three of Mustapha's sons are ministers. Riccardo, the eldest, claims that the transformation in their family stems from Jackie. "My mother always had Christ in her heart," he says, adding that, up until the miracle that brought Jackie back to life, the rest of the family only had Christ in their heads. It was the miracle of healing which brought about the transformation of their hearts.

STEPPING OUT IN FAITH

I have stood at the bedside of people with cancer more times than I like to remember. Cancer is like a malevolent presence that spreads, sometimes slowly, sometimes with amazing rapidity, throughout the body, feeding on the healthy cells of vital organs, the lungs, and even the brain. There are many homeopathic remedies to strengthen a person's immune system against cancer, but once the cancer cells begin to spread, medical science has only two remedies: radical surgery or radiation to remove the malignancy and/or killing the cancer cells (and often healthy cells) by injections of powerful chemicals in a process known as chemotherapy.

Surgery is usually successful in cases of prostate or breast cancer, where the malignancy is contained. Chemotherapy is often successful when the cancer is not too advanced. But when the cancer metastasizes rapidly to other parts of the body, only a miracle of God will avert death.

Mark Gravell never thought much about cancer. He had always been healthy. After all, he was only thirty years old, so he ignored the fatigue he began experiencing in his work as a courier. He was single and still living with his parents, Lynn and Vi Gravell, in their family home in Minneapolis.

Cancer is as silent as it is deadly. Mark didn't notice anything unusual about his health until a mole under his right arm began to grow and eventually bleed. If it had not been for the presence of the mole, Mark would have attributed his fatigue to overwork, lack of sleep, or poor diet. But just to be on the safe side, he went to his doctor to have the mole checked.

The doctor removed the mole and sent it to the pathology lab for routine testing. When the results came back, Mark listened to his doctor in stunned disbelief. This was not just a simple mole, nor was it a simple skin cancer. Mark Gravell had stage four melanoma!

The news got much, much worse. Further tests revealed that the cancer had spread to Mark's liver, spleen, and bones. It was so advanced that the very best of modern medical technology had little to offer.

Mark remembers, "Because I had waited so long to go to the doctor, the cancer was so far spread that almost all of their treatment options were experimental." The best treatment, Mark learned, even if successful, would only extend his life for a short while.

Mark's parents were devastated by the news. He was their only son, and the thought of losing him was more than they could bear. Mark's mother, Vi, says, "I felt like my heart had broken into a million pieces. My life had totally collapsed."

His father, Lynn, wanted it straight from the doctor without embellishment. "I said, 'If he did as you suggest, how much would that add to his life?' And the doctor said, 'I don't know exactly.' I said, 'Are we talking about a month or a few years?' And he said, 'A few months at most.'"

Despite the dire predictions of the doctors, Mark held on to his faith. He felt that God had given him the Twenty-third Psalm as a special promise. As he tells it, "That became what I held on to. When I was feeling low, or I was feeling scared, that was what I held on to because

God had said that I would be OK. This literally was the shadow of death cast over my life, but I believed in God."

The doctors prescribed a barrage of complex and expensive treatments. Mark decided to wait. He and his parents went to prayer, and they recruited everyone they knew to pray—at home and overseas. Mark's condition continued to decline. He couldn't keep food down and needed morphine to ease the excruciating pain. Like Abraham of old, Mark "contrary to hope, in hope believed" (Romans 4:18).

The pain was terrible. As he describes it, "It was very painful to move because of the lower back pain and the pelvic pain. It was almost like my bones were broken."

Mark's condition grew more and more hopeless, but like Mark, his parents felt that they had a promise from God. His father recalls, "I was sitting praying and I said to God, 'I don't want to lose my son.' He spoke back to me and said, 'I lost My Son too.' And I said, 'Yes, You did, but You raised Him up again.' And He said, 'Your son shall also live.'"

But that was not the only word upon which their faith rested. With tears in her eyes, Mark's mother, Vi, recalls a story she heard in church about a master chess player studying a painting called *Checkmate*. The master looked intently at the picture and made a startling pronouncement. "This picture is wrong," he said. "The king has one more move."

The pastor then said to the audience where Vi was sitting, "There's someone here tonight who thinks they're in checkmate, but God wants you to know the King has one more move!"

No one can claim that the road to a miracle healing of cancer is easy. Mark's parents rehearsed to themselves over and over God's promises as Mark got progressively worse. The tumor had grown larger than a softball. He was bedridden and had lost the use of his right arm. The night before his scheduled chemotherapy, Mark's faith wavered.

"I was able to hang on to the faith until the very end," he says. "The symptoms were as bad as they could be. I was bedridden, and the oncologist told me that I needed to start chemotherapy tomorrow if I was going to have any chance at all. I could not hold out anymore."

Mark and his father, deeply burdened by the enormity of the decision facing them, put the matter in God's hands. Mark vividly remembers that fateful night. "I said, 'You know what? I'll decide tomorrow morning. I'll give God one more night. But I have to feel significantly better tomorrow morning, or I'm going for the chemo.'"

That night, the King made His move. By morning, the miracle had begun. According to Mark, "I felt good enough that day not to take the morphine, the antinausea drugs, or the other prescription drugs. That's the first time in close to three months I didn't use any painkiller. That's how dramatic it was. I knew something had happened. My faith had been stretched. I had stepped out on faith alone, and it worked!"

That same week, Mark attended a prayer service where God put the finishing touches on his healing. The pain went away completely, and Mark was able to eat for the first time in six weeks and hold everything down.

Every symptom completely disappeared, and Mark soon returned to work. The tumor eventually faded away. He recently underwent a complete physical and received a clean bill of health.

Mark believes that two things brought about his healing—faith in God and prayer. "We prayed, and I stepped out in faith," he says. "That was the critical turning point when I came to the end within myself and I had to go one step further. God saw that, and He honored that faith.

"As far as the power of prayer," he continues, "it moves mountains, because I came across a big mountain in my life, and it was moved and cast into the sea."

He Heals the Sick

THE THREE COMPONENTS OF MIRACLE POWER

I believe that Mark's miracle healing is not just for him, but for everyone who hears of it. To be sure, Mark and his parents will for the rest of their lives be filled with praise to God for what He did in Mark's life. Mark's healing instructs us all.

The primary component of miracle power is *faith in God*. The source of faith is the Word of God or a word from God. "Faith *comes* by hearing, and hearing by the word of God" (Romans 10:17). Mark had a word from the Twenty-third Psalm. His father, Lynn, had a direct word from the Holy Spirit: "Your son shall live." His mother, Vi, had a message from the Holy Spirit given as a prophetic utterance by the pastor of a church.

The next component of a miracle is *a prayer of faith followed by human action*. Mark had to resist the judgment of doctors who wanted to prolong his life for only a few months by poisoning his cells with strong chemicals. His act of faith was to hold on to the very end—to give God "one more night."

Third, the miracle happens when *God's power answers our prayers and meets our act of faith*. On the last morning—this dying, pain-racked young man was set free by God's power. What God did for Mark, He can do for you—now!

DESIRE THE BETTER GIFTS

In this book, we have been looking at God's miraculous work among His people, learning from the example of Jesus and rejoicing with many people who have experienced God's supernatural activity in their lives. As we come to the end of our discussion on how miracles can be yours today, I want to share with you what I believe is the most important chapter in this book.

I can't even begin to plumb the depths of what I want to say in a single chapter—perhaps this is the subject for another book. But I want to share with you some information that will help you catch a glimpse of God's miraculous kingdom. This may be new information for some of you, but don't be distracted. Stay with me to the end of this chapter, and you'll catch a glimpse of the incredible, supernatural activity that God intends us to experience—not someday, in heaven, but here . . . today!

THE WEAPONS OF THE HOLY SPIRIT

The early Christian church faced what seemed to be insurmountable odds. They had no money and no material resources, so their physical survival required ongoing, everyday provision. "Give us this day our daily bread" had a very real significance to each of them. They had little formal education, so it was necessary that God teach them in a supernatural way.

They had few, if any, rights as Jews in the Roman Empire. In fact, the Roman Empire turned against them and began to arrest and persecute them. Every day, they needed supernatural ability to escape capture and defend themselves before hostile governmental authorities.

Every day, they faced hostile practitioners of Judaism and pagan cults, who viewed them as threats, not worthy of continued life. Every day, Satan and a host of demons were seeking to hinder them, discourage them, confuse them, and ultimately destroy them.

The apostle Paul put it well when he told the Christians at Antioch in Syria, "We must through much *tribulation* enter into the kingdom of God" (Acts 14:22 KJV; emphasis added). The Greek word Paul used is *thlipsis*, which literally means "pressures." These early Christians would, through many pressures, tribulations, and testings, live out their lives on earth as citizens of the kingdom of God.

Jesus Christ knew full well what His followers were facing. He was sending them out, a tiny band of brothers and sisters, into a hostile world that they were instructed to transform. They were to go into all the earth and teach all nations, teaching them to observe all things that He had commanded them, and to bring about a radical change of the culture and the lives of the people in the culture (Matthew 28:19–20).

For this task, Jesus gave His disciples an arsenal of weapons. Of course, He was not giving them swords or bows and arrows or siege machines, but the weapons of the Holy Spirit. That is why He emphatically forbade them to begin the task until they had been endued with "power from on high" (Luke 24:49). The task before them required the awesome miracle-working power of God, and this is exactly what Jesus Christ gave to His people then and continues to give to His people now.

POWER FROM ON HIGH

There are two words in the Greek New Testament that our English Bibles traditionally translate "power." But the meaning is dramatically different.

The first word is *dunamis*, from which the English word *dynamite* is derived. *Dunamis* is inherent explosive force. Jesus told His little flock, "You shall receive power [*dunamis,* resident explosive force] when the Holy Spirit has come upon you" (Acts 1:8). Those Christians would have a force inside of them that would be greater than all of the *thlipsis* with which the world system would pressure them. They clearly recognized this fact and boldly proclaimed, "Greater is he that is in you, than he that is in the world" (1 John 4:4 KJV).

This was the power to heal the sick, to cast out demons, to still the storms of life. With the baptism of the Holy Spirit, Christians are given resident explosive force. Today, we have only the vaguest concept of how much power is available to us. After all, this is the power that the Father activated when He created the universe. How much of it has been given to us we don't know for sure, but we do know that a speck of it—a "mustard seed," as Jesus said—inside us is enough to empower our words to cause mountains to move (Luke 17:6).

This is why Christians must constantly refuse those who think that Christianity consists merely of assent to some creedal statement and the observance of a set of rules and regulations. Christianity is life and joy and power in the Holy Spirit, not words and regulations (Galatians 3:1–5). It is a transformed life where we are seated with God "in heavenly places in Christ Jesus" (Ephesians 2:6 KJV). It is liberation: "Where the

Spirit of the Lord is there is liberty" (2 Corinthians 3:17). It is being led by the Holy Spirit: "As many as are led by the Spirit of God, they are the sons of God" (Romans 8:14). It is a life of power: "You will receive power when the Holy Spirit has come upon you" (Acts 1:8).

AUTHORITY TO OVERCOME THE ENEMY

In addition to resident power, Jesus also gave to His disciples authority. The Greek word *exousia* in the King James Bible has been translated "power." But *exousia* is a vastly different type of power from that of *dunamis*.

The hydrogen bombs that scientists created have power that defies rational calculations. It is resident explosive force sufficient to destroy cities, nations, even all of civilization. Yet the authority to deploy that awesome power has been placed, with certain safeguards, in the hands of the president of the United States. A president can be a scrawny weakling or a man with great physical strength. Neither would be relevant. What is relevant is that the person who holds that office has been given the authority to act on behalf of the three hundred million citizens of a great nation. Power resides in the bombs. Authority to use the bombs resides with the duly elected representative of the nation.

Jesus Christ gave His disciples *"authority . . .* to overcome all the *power* of the enemy; nothing will harm you. However, do not rejoice that the spirits submit to you, but rejoice that your names are written in heaven" (Luke 10:19–20 NIV; emphasis added).

Here Jesus gives His disciples authority (*exousia*) over all the power (*dunamis*) of the enemy. He did not necessarily give them more absolute resident ability than Satan, but Jesus gave them the necessary authority to speak on His behalf in order to nullify the power of Satan and his fallen angels.

When we pray in Jesus's name, when we command demonic forces in Jesus's name, we are exercising the authority of the One who said before He departed for heaven, *"All authority in heaven and on earth has been given to me. Therefore go and make disciples of all nations, baptizing them in the name of the Father and of the Son and of the Holy Spirit, and teaching them to obey everything I have commanded you. And surely I am with you always, to the very end of the age"* (Matthew 28:18–20 NIV; emphasis added).

The sweep of His authority is awesome. Jesus Christ has authority over all the angels; He has authority over the devil and all his minions; He has authority on earth over every emperor, king, president, prime minister, legislator, judge, cabinet officer, military commander, and officer. Other than the Father Himself, there is no other god or man who is not subject to Jesus's authority. Jesus has all authority, and in His administration of the earth, He has delegated the ongoing declaration of His authority into the hands of Christian believers all over the world!

It comes as a sobering realization to believers that they hold in their hands the authority to restrict satanic power and, in the process, to stop abortion, to stop pornography, to change governments, to prevent war, to alleviate human suffering, and to call for angels to give "open skies" over entire regions for the preaching of the gospel in furtherance of Jesus's mandate.

THE GIFTS OF REVELATION

Our mandate of authority is awesome beyond comprehension, but so are the weapons of *dunamis* power that Jesus has made available to each Spirit-filled believer. These spiritual weapons are called manifestations, or "gifts" of the Holy Spirit. In the Bible, they are called *charismata*, which means the expression of *charis*, or grace. They are the something extra that God, in His grace, extends to His children.

165

The apostle Paul in 1 Corinthians 12 lists *charismata*, or gifts of the Holy Spirit, divided into three groups of three. These special enablements are manifestations of revelation, manifestations of utterance, and manifestations of power. Spirit-filled believers may receive the gift of revelation in multiple ways—a word of wisdom, a word of knowledge, or discerning of spirits.

Word of Wisdom

Solomon had heightened intelligence and common sense to make wise decisions. This is wisdom. But the "word of wisdom" goes beyond and provides a specific glimpse of the future.

Each year end, I set aside a time of prayer that God would give me insight into the coming year so that I might order the affairs of His ministry in a manner pleasing to Him. What He has shown me year by year has been remarkable. For example, in the December prior to the first Gulf War, the Lord told me that the war would be swift, that casualties would be light, and that President George Bush would be hailed as a hero. He also told me that the stock market would go up.

I arranged a meeting with the president and arrived at the White House when television news was announcing the breakdown of talks in Geneva between Iraqi Foreign Minister Tariq Aziz and Secretary of State James Baker. I delivered the message of hope and victory to the president. We joined our hands, and I prayed God's blessing on him. I departed out one door of the Oval Office. He went out another door to the Cabinet Room, where the assembled group determined that Saddam Hussein should be expelled by force from Kuwait.

As the war unfolded, victory came swiftly. Casualties were light. In the middle of the action, the United States stock market made a dramatic jump. What the Lord had told me happened precisely as He had said!

Of all the gifts of the Holy Spirit, I believe the word of wisdom is the most precious. With it we can see ahead to avoid pitfalls, to be warned of danger, to learn of future opportunities, to gain insight into the world around us.

To the average person, foretelling future events is usually called "prophecy." Christians can give a prophecy that contains a word of wisdom concerning the future, but prophecy as a gift of the Holy Spirit is not primarily concerned with future events.

Word of Knowledge

The second manifestation of revelation available to believers is called the "word of knowledge." As the first is not wisdom, but *a word of wisdom*, even so this is not knowledge, but *a word of knowledge*. This is a gift that my cohosts and I have experienced thousands of times as we have prayed on television.

What is a word of knowledge? It is a revelation by the Holy Spirit to the inner man of something that may not be learned by the senses. This knowledge does not come from sight, hearing, taste, touch, or smell. It certainly is not some psychic experience. It is a word from the Lord about something that is usually a present, but unknown, reality. The word can come like a soft voice within us, or it can activate the senses. When a manifestation like this is used for God's glory, the resulting blessing in the life of a suffering person can be beyond calculation.

Consider the case of a Jewish welder named David Varon. David, in his own words, was "a wild man, a welder . . . completely antisocial, separated from the world by my own desires." David was big and burly, with a bushy beard and wild, unkempt hair.

A decade ago, David, who owned a gold mine in Arizona, was focused on three things: gold, power, and himself. Then a welding accident changed his life. "I was working on a piece of equipment, and I was using a carbon arc torch, which sprays out molten steel," he said. "And it went through the side of my helmet. The molten metal went right through the blue part of my eye and put out my vision."

To most of us, such a horrible accident would have sent us into shock. Not so with David Varon, who announced matter of factly, "Being a mountain man, I just figured I had another eye. I was just going to ride this thing out. Big deal, I lost one of my eyes."

But this injury was a big deal—a very serious problem. David continues, "The next day it was worse and started getting infected. So by the end of the second day, I knew I was in trouble. The infection started going into my good eye, and I was so dizzy from the infection that I knew it was going into my brain. It was now going to destroy my right eye, which was the only thing I had left."

David, the tough mountain man, knew he needed medical attention and fast. As he dressed to go to the hospital, he absentmindedly flipped on the television. The *700 Club* was on, and David walked to the television set to turn it off. I was the host of the program and was praying for the audience. Before David Varon could flip the switch, he heard words come from my mouth that he says "really stunned" him.

Remember, I do not live in Arizona. I do not know David Varon. I knew nothing of his accident, and I had no idea that he was watching the program. But here is the exact word that I spoke that day under the inspiration of the Holy Spirit:

There's somebody, it may have been an industrial accident or it may have been a home accident, but there is a piece of metal, I believe, that went into somebody's eye and I presume it's been taken out, but I don't know. Whatever it is, that wound is going to be healed, that piece of material is going to come out by the power of God, and your eye is going to be miraculously healed in Jesus's name! Amen.

When the name of Jesus was mentioned, David says that, because he is Jewish, he hurried to the TV and turned it off. But David could not push a button and get rid of the God of Abraham, Isaac, and Jacob. God had given a word of knowledge, and His word would stand.

The nearest hospital to his remote mine was seventy miles away, so David got into his battered pickup truck and headed down the road. Then the miracle happened!

"I started driving," he recalls, "and I was feeling pretty sick from the infection. And so then I started feeling good, then I started feeling very good! My eye became really warm, so I slowed the truck down and I looked in the mirror. I'm looking at a destroyed eye and *phew!* out came the metal! And there was a perfectly normal eye where there was a very bad-looking thing before. The eye was immediately all right. It looked just like my other eye—except for a white, tiny scar where the metal came out."

David Varon, a Jewish, self-described "wild, mountain man," had just received a miracle through a word of knowledge from a person he had never met who was fifteen hundred miles away broadcasting on television. The word was given in the name of Jesus the Messiah. The metal really did pop out—the eye really was instantly healed—and David knew the time had come for serious reflection. He pondered for a week. Just what had happened to him?

David needed someone to talk to about the questions burning in his mind. So David called a man he had just met, Shelly Volk, the pastor of a Messianic Jewish congregation. David says Shelly "explained to me

Jesus; he explained to me salvation, and forgiveness of sins. I knew I was a bad sinner and I needed forgiveness. So I listened to Shelly. I listened to him very well."

David and Shelly did more than talk. Shelly prayed for David and then led him in the sinner's prayer. As Shelly tells it, "So at that moment, in our dining room, David became a member of the kingdom of God and accepted Yeshua—Jesus—as his Lord and Savior."

Today, ten years later, David is eternally grateful for a word of knowledge that not only healed his eyesight but brought the light of God's love into his spirit. He says, "There was nothing good about me back then. Now I know that the good that's in me and flows out of me isn't me; it's Jesus; it's Yeshua. And He's given me a totally different life."

Discerning of Spirits

A third manifestation of revelation given to the church to carry out Jesus's mission to all the nations is called "discerning of spirits."

In the early days of His ministry, Jesus was in the process of selecting twelve men, later known as apostles, who would be charged with the task of carrying on the work when Jesus returned to the Father. He called into His service Andrew and then his brother Simon, later called Peter. Then He called Philip, from the town of Bethsaida, who, in turn, brought his brother, Nathanael, to Jesus.

When Jesus saw Nathanael approach, He "discerned Nathanael's spirit" and said, "Here is a true Israelite, in whom there is nothing false" (John 1:47 NIV). Nathanael responded, "How do you know me?" (v. 48 NIV).

Each of us has a spirit. The real you is your spirit. Our spirit is housed in a body with a mind through which we present ourselves to the outside world. Most people wear some sort of a mask that covers the real person. Others are very open and are often described as "transparent." Some are said to wear their heart on their sleeves.

In our age, transparent people are few and far between. The mask wearers predominate. Discerning of spirits is an empowerment of the Holy Spirit that enables certain Christians to see past all the facades to the real spirit at the core of other human beings. I can't fully describe how incredibly useful such an ability would be in spiritual counseling, or for that matter in traversing the hidden deceit that often comes up in our everyday human contacts.

Of course, the broader principle underlying the gift of discerning spirits is the ability to pierce the veil that separates human beings from the spiritual world that surrounds us—where God is, where angels are, and where devils are. We think back to the words of Jesus to Nicodemus, a member of the Jewish Sanhedrin, who came seeking insight into God's manner of dealing with human beings. "Except a man be born again," Jesus said, "he cannot see the kingdom of God" (John 3:3 KJV).

For miracles to take place in our lives, we must have the faith that reaches beyond the so-called practical reality of what is considered possible in the visible world. Faith is the evidence of what we can't see. Faith reaches beyond the visible to the invisible world—the secret kingdom—where all things are possible.

The Bible tells us a wonderful story out of the life of the ancient Hebrew prophet Elisha that perfectly illustrates the gift of discerning spirits.

We learn that in the struggle between the early kings of Israel and the kings of Aram (an ancient name for Syria), raiding parties from Aram would make incursions into northern Israel. Time and again, God told the prophet Elisha the Aramean battle plans, through what the New Testament would consider a "word of wisdom"; and time and again, Elisha would warn the king of Israel, who was able to take appropriate measure to block the Arameans' plans.

Finally, the king of Aram realized that he was not dealing with a spy among his trusted advisers, but a prophet of the Lord. Consequently, the king of Aram demanded to know where Elisha was. When he learned that Elisha was in Dothan, he sent a large force across the border that surrounded Dothan.

When Elisha's assistant went out the next morning, he was terrified and ran inside to tell Elisha the frightening news that their little town was surrounded by hostile forces. Elisha calmly surveyed the situation and said, "Don't be afraid. Those who are with us are more than those who are with them" (2 Kings 6:16 NIV).

The assistant was still quaking with fear, so Elisha prayed that in that instant the assistant would be permitted discerning of spirits. "'O LORD, open his eyes so he may see.' Then the LORD opened the servant's eyes, and he looked and saw the hills full of horses and chariots of fire all around Elisha" (v. 17 NIV).

The angels had always been there in times of peril. Elisha could see them, but his assistant was not able to see until the Lord granted him for that instant one of the weapons that Jesus Christ has made available to His church—discerning of spirits.

Many who read the enumeration of spiritual gifts (or *charismata*) in 1 Corinthians 12 believe that the apostle termed this gift "discerning of spirits" (v. 10). The world of spirits includes human spirits, angelic spirits, spirits of devils, and the Spirit of the Lord. Everyday impressions—often called "leadings"—come into our mind. Are these impressions arising from our carnal nature, or from our own spirit, or from Satan and demon spirits, or from other human spirits, or from the Holy Spirit of God? Spiritual maturity is in large measure defined by our ability to know the difference, by our ability to respond in obedience to the Spirit of God and to reject with alacrity what comes from sources not of God.

The gifts of revelation are of great value to Christians who wish to be used by God to serve others.

THE GIFTS OF UTTERANCE

This brings us to the second set of weapons of power that Jesus Christ gave to His church, the gifts of utterance. Again, there are three gifts of utterance—messages in tongues, interpretation of tongues, and messages in prophecy.

Prophecy

The apostle Paul exhorts us to "eagerly desire spiritual gifts, especially the gift of prophecy" (1 Corinthians 14:1 NIV). As I have already explained, prophecy, as one of the New Testament *charismata*, is not telling the future. In 1 Corinthians 14, we learn that prophecy is to edify the church (v. 4); is for believers, not for unbelievers (v. 22); and is given for edification, exhortation, and comfort (v. 3).

An exhortation given under the power of the Holy Spirit is intended to challenge the church for renewed zeal in the same manner that a college football coach exhorts his players at halftime to fight a good fight and win the game.

Edification means building up. Prophecy rightly given should build up faith, courage, hope, and endurance. It should strengthen the church members in their love of God and their love of each other. The English word *comfort* comes from Latin and French roots meaning "with strength." The comfort that the apostle Paul describes in 1 Corinthians 14:3 means primarily a consolation or solace. Prophecy can console Christians who are sad or have suffered hurts, insults, or losses.

Think what strength comes to a congregation when one of their members is truly filled with the Spirit of the Lord and begins to speak in His name a message like this: "Thus says the Lord, 'The enemy has attacked you and caused you grief. I have heard your prayers, and I know your sorrow. Now the day of sorrow has ended, and a time of blessing has begun. Rise up and build, for the day of harvest has arrived.'"

Church sermons are a good thing, as is inspired teaching from the Bible. But imagine how electric a church service can be when the Holy Spirit speaks not just through one pastor, but through various members—where there is a demonstration of the word of knowledge—where people's spiritual and material needs are being miraculously met—where the people are hearing words directly from the Holy Spirit!

I want to give one word of caution at this point, however. The Bible tells us, "Despise not prophesyings" (1 Thessalonians 5:20 KJV). Obviously, the reason that this warning was placed in the Bible was that members of the early church were despising prophecy, since a good portion of it was bogus. It is easy for church meetings to be taken over by those who are intent on trying to control the membership by couching their own points of view in a manner as if the message is coming from God Himself. The Bible says, "The spirits of the prophets are subject to the prophets" (1 Corinthians 14:32). There must be decency and order in church services, along with intelligent leaders who are clearly led by the Holy Spirit. Otherwise, chaos develops.

On the day of Pentecost that followed Jesus's resurrection, the small, fearful band of early Christians were baptized with the Holy Spirit as Jesus had both commanded and promised. On that wonderful day, there was transformation as the Holy Spirit filled the Upper Room, where they had been praying. There was the sound of a rushing wind. The two words used in the Bible for "spirit" can also be translated "wind" or "breath." Our term for air-filled devices, *pneumatic*, comes from the Greek *pneuma*, which is translated "spirit" in the New Testament.

The symbol of holiness in the Bible is fire. On the day of Pentecost, tongues of fire appeared on the heads of each believer. Fire for *holy*, and wind for *spirit*. The reaction of the disciples to this encounter was to speak in other languages as the Spirit gave them utterance. They burst forth from that encounter praising God. Strangers from all over the Mediterranean heard them speaking in foreign languages, glorifying and magnifying God.

Once a person has been baptized in the Holy Spirit, as took place on that special day of Pentecost, he or she can pray at will in the Spirit. The apostle Paul said, "I will pray with my spirit, but I will also pray with my mind; I will sing with my spirit, but I will also sing with my mind. . . . I thank God that I speak in tongues more than all of you. But in the church I would rather speak five intelligible words to instruct others than ten thousand words in a tongue" (1 Corinthians 14:15, 18–19 NIV).

Communicating in Tongues

The second and third gifts of utterance are bringing a message in tongues and interpreting that message. A message in tongues that is interpreted so that it can be understood is equivalent to prophecy and should have the same purposes—exhortation, edification, and comfort. The apostle Paul tells us that praying in tongues is private buildup of a believer's spirit, but prophecy edifies the entire church (1 Corinthians 14:4).

Of course, two gifts of the Holy Spirit can be in operation at the same time. The Holy Spirit can bring into our mind a word of wisdom that foretells the future. That revelation can be included in a message that the Holy Spirit gives to edify a body of believers. The full operation of God's wonderful power opens up vistas of ministry, making the life of a Christian one of excitement and joy.

The final three weapons that Jesus Christ gave to His church from the day of Pentecost until the end of the age are the gifts of healing, working of miracles, and miracle faith.

Healing

Note that the Bible tells us of "gifts of" healing, not a "gift to" heal. Gifts of healing are for sick people. The one carrying them is like a postman delivering packages. The gifts of healing depend on the faith of the recipient to receive the gift as well as the faith of the one delivering it. If an individual had a gift "to heal," then he or she should be able to restore to health everyone in a hospital regardless of their spiritual condition. This is not the purpose of the healing gift.

Miracles

This is a book devoted to miracles, but in a technical sense, the *charismata* for healings is differentiated from the *charismata* for miracles. Here is what I mean.

Evangelist T. L. Osborne experienced amazing healings and miracles in his storied ministry overseas. He told us of an incident that occurred during a crusade meeting in Ghana, West Africa. A large crowd of two hundred thousand people had gathered for the outdoor meeting to hear Osborne preach on faith and the power of Jesus Christ. On the very outskirts of the crowd was a man leaning on crutches whose leg was severed below the knee. As T. L. Osborne preached, the Holy Spirit moved among the crowd, and the gift of miracles began to be in operation.

Faith began to rise in the heart of the man with the missing leg. Suddenly, the bones began to grow, then the muscles, and the nerves, arteries, blood vessels, flesh, and skin. Then an ankle was formed, then a foot with the toes and toenails. A creative miracle had occurred for this man missing a leg and foot. It all grew back as good as new. This was clearly a miracle.

In the previous chapter, I related stories of healings that we consider miraculous. What is the difference between a healing and a miracle? Obviously they overlap, but in the interest of clarity consider this: You cut your finger with a sharp knife. You immediately cleanse the wound and apply an antiseptic, then a Band-Aid. If asked how the cut is, you would be perfectly correct to say, "It is healing." If prayer is offered, the process might accelerate dramatically and the wound would close instantly, or the natural process of healing might take longer. Whether instant or gradual, as soon as infection was removed, a healing took place.

If a new lung, a new kidney, a new eye, or a new arm or leg is formed by prayer and action of God's power, that is a miracle. The activation of an immune system, along with the destruction of cancer cells and the formation of new cells is a healing miracle. Terms and definitions don't matter. What does matter is the ability for good that God has placed in the hands of His people!

Faith

Finally, the Bible lists "faith" as both a charismatic enablement and as a fruit of the indwelling Holy Spirit (1 Corinthians 12:9). How can faith be both a fruit of the Spirit (Galatians 5:22) and a gift of the Spirit?

When the Lord told me to leave New York and go to Virginia with seventy dollars to buy a television station, a supernatural presence came upon me that made a supernatural undertaking seem completely possible. This was clearly a demonstration of the gift of faith. It was instant and beyond the scope of my everyday experiences and expectations.

On the other hand, I have seen faith as a fruit of the Holy Spirit, growing day by day as I and our staff learned day by day to believe God for our "daily bread." Over the years, the ministry numbers have gotten bigger, and our faith grows each year to believe God to meet the needs of a larger and larger enterprise. First it was $8,000 a year; then $20,000; then $100,000; then $500,000; then $1 million; and after forty-five years, more than $400 million each year for all of the outreach, including a relief organization, Operation Blessing. This is the result of faith, the fruit of the Spirit.

MIRACLES CAN BE YOURS TODAY!

The Bible tells us to earnestly desire these "better gifts" of the Spirit. You see, your life is not an accident. Your daily activities are not random. King David testified, "All the days ordained for me were written in [God's] book before one of them came to be" (Psalm 139:16 NIV). Job pondered in awe, "Does [God] not see my ways and count my every step?" (Job 31:4 NIV). Every nanosecond of your life has been known to God long before you were born. There is a plan for your life!

What is God's plan for you today? *To partner with Him to see miracles happen in your life and the lives of others around you.* You have the awesome privilege today of being His instrument to transfer the life-changing power of his invisible "miraculous kingdom" into your visible, down-to-earth world. Think about it. When you lay your head on the pillow tonight, you should be able to think back with great joy and satisfaction, saying, "God used me today to demonstrate His miracle-working power."

I'm not just talking about God working through your faith to see dead people raised, sight restored to the blind, quadriplegics walking and leaping, and so on. Yes, God can partner with you to perform awesome, Book-of-Acts miracles like these. But I'm also talking about the many,

many miracles we can perform daily which may not be as spectacular but are just as awesome as anything Jesus or the apostles did. You have the exciting opportunity today to participate in countless numbers of miraculous events, whether you see the miracle happen or not. But your participation requires the awesome power of God provided to you through the gifts of the Spirit. That's the crucial role of these "better gifts" in the lives of believers.

After His resurrection, Jesus met His disciples on the shores of the Sea of Galilee where He had built a fire and was cooking fish. "Come and dine," He invited His disciples then (John 21:12). And He invites us now: "Come and dine."

There is a treasure trove of miraculous blessings for you. Miracle power awaits you. Earnestly desire it. Hunger and thirst after it. Keep on asking. Keep on seeking. If you ask, you will receive. If you seek, you will find.

Miracles can be yours today. Come and dine!